Cambridge Elei

Elements in Political Econc
edited by
David Stasavage
New York University

REFORMING TO SURVIVE

The Bolshevik Origins of Social Policies

Magnus B. Rasmussen
University of South-Eastern Norway

Carl Henrik Knutsen
University of Oslo

CAMBRIDGE
UNIVERSITY PRESS

Shaftesbury Road, Cambridge CB2 8EA, United Kingdom

One Liberty Plaza, 20th Floor, New York, NY 10006, USA

477 Williamstown Road, Port Melbourne, VIC 3207, Australia

314–321, 3rd Floor, Plot 3, Splendor Forum, Jasola District Centre,
New Delhi – 110025, India

103 Penang Road, #05–06/07, Visioncrest Commercial, Singapore 238467

Cambridge University Press is part of Cambridge University Press & Assessment,
a department of the University of Cambridge.

We share the University's mission to contribute to society through the pursuit of
education, learning and research at the highest international levels of excellence.

www.cambridge.org
Information on this title: www.cambridge.org/9781108995474

DOI: 10.1017/9781108983334

First published 2022

A catalogue record for this publication is available from the British Library.

ISBN 978-1-108-99547-4 Paperback
ISSN 2398-4031 (online)
ISSN 2514-3816 (print)

Reforming to Survive

The Bolshevik Origins of Social Policies

Elements in Political Economy

DOI: 10.1017/9781108983334
First published online: December 2022

Magnus B. Rasmussen
University of South-Eastern Norway

Carl Henrik Knutsen
University of Oslo

Author for correspondence: Magnus B. Rasmussen,
magnus.rasmussen@usn.no

Abstract: This Element details how elites provide policy concessions when they face credible threats of revolution. Specifically, the authors discuss how the Bolshevik Revolution of 1917 and the subsequent formation of Comintern enhanced elites' perceptions of revolutionary threat by affecting the capacity and motivation of labor movements as well as the elites' interpretation of information signals. These developments incentivized elites to provide policy concessions to urban workers, notably reduced working hours and expanded social transfer programs. The authors assess their argument by using original qualitative and quantitative data. First, they document changes in perceptions of revolutionary threat and strategic policy concessions in early inter-war Norway by using archival and other sources. Second, they code, for example, representatives at the 1919 Comintern meeting to proxy for credibility of domestic revolutionary threat in cross-national analysis. States facing greater threats expanded various social policies to a larger extent than other countries, and some of these differences persisted for decades.

Keywords: revolution, welfare state, labor regulations, Communism, Norway

This project has received funding from the European Research Council (ERC) under the European Union's Horizon 2020 research and innovation programme (grant agreement No 863486)

ISBNs: 9781108995474 (PB), 9781108983334 (OC)
ISSNs: 2398-4031 (online), 2514-3816 (print)

Contents

Further Online Appendix can be accessed at
www.cambridge.org/Rasmussen_online appendix

1 Introduction

The ice has been broken. The Soviets have won all round the world. They have won first of all and above all in the sense that they have won the sympathies of the proletarian masses. . ... The new movement advances towards the dictatorship of the proletariat. . ... The foundation of the third international, of the Communist International, is the prelude to an International Soviet Republic.

Lenin, March 5, 1919 (quoted in Pons, 2014, 7)

No, this has nothing to do with communism or socialism.
If it is anything, it is policy aimed at the preservation of society!

Odd Klingenberg (1923) Norwegian Minister of Social Affairs (Conservative)
commenting on the introduction of old-age pensions

The Bolshevik Revolution in Russia in 1917 marks the beginning of what Hobsbawm (1994) labels the "short 20th century," characterized by the world being divided into a capitalist and a communist sphere. Yet, the Bolshevik Revolution – led by revolutionaries with aspirations far beyond Russia – also constituted a threat to elites as well as other social groups in capitalist countries; it was a symbolic event and learning experience for revolutionaries across the world (Pons, 2014). The Bolsheviks also promised ideological and logistic support to revolutionaries outside Russia. This contributed to split many labor movements between reformist and revolutionary groups, with the formation of several new communist parties (Berman, 2006; Lipset, 1983). In this Element, we propose that these developments, and the resulting new threats to the political and economic orders cherished by elites in different countries, helped shape policymaking even in countries that remained staunchly capitalist. We present different pieces of corroborating evidence for this proposition. Primarily, we present evidence from early-twentieth-century Norway – a country where elites faced severe revolutionary threats from "the left" in the aftermath of the Bolshevik Revolution. We also present various cross-country analyses drawing on original data from countries across the world.

Previous theoretical and empirical work (Acemoglu & Robinson, 2000, 2006; Aidt & Jensen, 2014; Przeworski, 2009) have highlighted how *revolutionary threats* by the poor may spur political inclusion, notably in the form of extended suffrage rights, and elaborated on the rational and cognitive mechanisms behind such processes (Weyland, 2010, 2014, 2019).[1] Other studies have documented that business elites' preferences for accepting redistributive policy is contingent on perceiving revolutionary threats (Paster, 2013). This observation could contribute to explain the finding that mass mobilization and

---

[1] Our focus on revolutionary threats differs from perspectives that consider actual revolutions and their impacts (Scheidel, 2018).

destruction during and following the world wars led to massive expansions in social spending (Obinger & Petersen, 2017; Obinger et al., 2018; Obinger & Schmitt, 2020). Previous work has also documented how social policy can be used to enhance regime legitimacy (e.g. Flora & Heidenheimer, 1982; Rimlinger, 1971), thereby potentially enhancing the durability of the political regime (Eibl, 2020; Knutsen & Rasmussen, 2018). There can also be international dimensions to such dynamics; notably, the competition between "East" and "West" during the Cold War increased political incentives for enacting generous social policies, in order to shore up internal support, in both camps (Obinger & Schmitt, 2011; Sant'Anna & Weller, 2020).

Integrating these different insights, we theorize and assess how revolutionary threats shape politics, and we focus on *policy change* as our outcome of interest, rather than regime change or inequality. Further, we move the focus from long-term legitimacy concerns and rather consider how social policy can be used to preempt immediate threats. We also go beyond focusing on business elites and broaden our scope to consider how various (political and economic) elites respond to revolutionary threats.[2] When doing so, we specify the different cognitive and rational mechanisms that may induce elites to expand social policy to mitigate perceived threats.

We embed this general argument in a particular context. Specifically, we address how developments following the Bolshevik Revolution – and especially after the formation of Comintern in 1919 – shaped social policies by spurring perceptions of credible revolutionary threats among elites, who responded with expanding social policies aimed at defusing the threat. Comintern participation by domestic worker organizations enhanced (perceptions of) working class revolutionary threats, potentially due to multiple mechanisms: First, the international network and Russian support that accompanied Comintern participation increased the capacity of domestic revolutionary actors and even helped spur new organizations with revolutionary potential. Second, participation in Comintern altered these groups' ideological outlook, if nothing else by strengthening more radical and revolutionary fractions. Third, working class organizations being invited by the Russians to attend Comintern functioned as an easy-to-identify informational cue that enhanced elite perceptions of a credible revolutionary threat.

The exact relevance of these channels notwithstanding, an increase in perceived revolutionary threat, here following the Bolshevik Revolution and subsequent formation of Comintern, induced elites to pursue large-scale

---

[2] By elites, we mean groups of wealthy or powerful individuals with intrinsic interests in maintaining the current political regime and economic system. See Section 2.1 for further elaboration.

expansions of social transfer programs, reduce working hours, etc., in order to appease the working classes and quell grievances that could fuel a revolution.

Our primary focus on revolutionary threats does, of course, *not* imply that other proposed determinants of redistributive policies and social transfer programs are irrelevant, even in the context of revolutionary threat. Some of these factors, such as suffrage extensions or the adoption of proportional representation (PR), may even be potential transmitters of (parts of) the relevant effect from revolutionary threat to policy change (Aidt & Jensen, 2014; Gjerløw & Rasmussen, 2022; Iversen, 2005; Iversen & Soskice, 2006). Yet other factors, such as war mobilization and cross-border policy diffusion, may be orthogonal (Obinger et al., 2018; Scheve & Stasavage, 2012, 2016). Further, the formation of the International Labor Organization (ILO) in 1919 likely also contributed to shifting governmental policy positions (Rasmussen, 2021), and in many (European) countries socialist parties entered government for the first time after World War I, enabling them to implement their programs into policy (Korpi, 1989, 2006). In our empirical analysis, we try to ensure that our relationship of interest is robust to accounting for such alternative explanations of policy change.

The empirical analysis presented in this Element is two-fold, comprising both an in-depth historical case study of Norway 1915–24 *and* cross-country analysis using different new proxies of revolutionary threats and various new measures of policy characteristics. These analyses provide complementary pieces of evidence – the case study gives ample material for carefully mapping the relevant mechanisms and the cross-country analysis is attuned to generalizability and assessing implications concerning "average treatment effects." By and large, these different pieces of evidence turn out to support our argument that fear of revolution pushed elites to extend various social policies, as concessions, after the Bolshevik Revolution.

For our case study, we draw on numerous archival sources and the work of historians to document perceptions on the likelihood of revolution from employer organizations, the police, military officers, and politicians, and their strategies for countering this threat. Admittedly, the Norwegian case is selected, in large part, because of "convenience reasons," predominantly the access to ample archival and other source material (the authors are native-Norwegian speakers), which is a requisite for carefully assessing our argument. Yet, the Norwegian case is also especially suited for our purposes of identifying the theorized mechanisms, since it expectedly scores high on our "treatment variable" of interest, revolutionary threat perceptions. In the late 1910s, radical elements achieved control of the labor movement and main social democratic party, which also joined the Comintern. Hence, Norway is likely a case in which we should spot our proposed mechanisms in action, *if* our theory is correct.

There are also other good reasons for zooming in on the Norwegian case. Major Norwegian welfare expansions, at least from the 1930s onwards, have typically been interpreted as resulting from social democratic reformism (Esping-Andersen & Korpi, 1986), the interests and negotiations between farmers and workers (Alestalo & Kuhnle, 1986; Baldwin, 1988, 1990; Manow, 2009), or cross-party welfare state consensus (Kuhnle, 1978). Insofar as these alternative driving forces are generally considered as the main factors behind social policy development, one might expect it to be harder to detect a strong and clear role for revolutionary threat perceptions (even if they were present) in driving policy and institutional change in Norway than in other cases. More importantly, pressures for social policy adoption were *not* directly tied to mobilization during World War I, as Norway remained neutral. Hence, selecting Norway as our main case mitigates one important potential source of confounding, namely mass mobilization (see Obinger et al., 2018; Scheve and Stasavage, 2016).[3]

We detail how Norwegian elites believed that workers truly could conduct a revolution in Norway following the Bolshevik Revolution. We show how institutional linkages between the Labor Party and Comintern, strike waves, and the formation of solider and worker councils, after 1919, helped shape this belief. Economic and political elites coordinated their response against this perceived revolutionary threat by using various stick-and-carrot tactics. We provide numerous and very clear statements from the main actors themselves (as well as several historians) as to their motivations for pursuing different reforms and policies, including their desire to mitigate the prospect of a revolution. We find this to be strong evidence that the perceived threat of a revolution was high, and directly contributed to several actions and policy changes.[4] Regarding the carrots, elites strategically pursued appeasement and inclusion of the nonrevolutionary faction of the Labor party and worker movement, implementing several reforms that they initially had opposed, notably including the eight-hour workday and electoral rule reform, which were economically and politically costly reforms for the elites to concede. Other changes included accepting a government-funded plan for socialization of all Norwegian firms, major expansions of sickness and unemployment benefits, a temporary act of company councils, and franchise expansion with the poor

---

[3] However, similarly to the Netherlands and other Scandinavian countries, Norway mobilized a neutrality guard during the war years.

[4] Granted, "perceived risk of revolution" is a continuous variable, and it is hard to pin down the exact level of the threat perception. Insofar as our theoretical argument is valid, we note that had the perceived threat level been even higher than what it was, it might very well be that Norwegian elites would have conceded even more in terms of policies and institutional changes, or enacted these changes even more rapidly, than they did.

relief reform of 1919. Some policies were enacted quite rapidly, whereas work on numerous other policies was started with promises of later legislation and implementation, also with the clear intention to appease radicals. Following our theoretical expectations, policy gains that had been conceded (and implemented) before the revolutionary fear dissipated (in 1923/24) proved persistent, whereas promised policies not yet passed were never implemented.

For our cross-country tests, we code and use new country-level measures on various social policies. Further, we code new proxies of revolutionary threat (perceptions), including on the formation of soldier and worker councils. Our main such measure draws on the observation that Trotsky, in January 1919, invited several revolutionary groups to set up Comintern in Moscow (Carr, 1979). Invitations did not include all labor organizations and were not random, but only sent to truly radical worker groups (to avoid "ideological contamination"). This feature allows us to distinguish contexts where labor had adopted a radical ideology from others. Not only should we consider these Russian invitations an "expert opinion" on which countries faced revolutionary pressures in 1918–19, they also provided clear signals to elites that domestic labor groups were revolutionary and had significant resources at their disposal. Countries facing such a clear threat, it turns out, were more likely to reduce working hours and pass more extensive and generous social policy reforms. Various panel regressions using alternative control strategies and instrumental variable analysis, corroborate this hypothesis. This revolutionary shock lingered on; states that experienced greater revolutionary threat in 1919 had lower working hours at the end of the Cold War. Further analysis of different plausible mechanisms suggests that this persistent relationship, in part, relates to the historical formation of Communist parties, linked to Comintern and funding from Moscow.

1.1 Roadmap of the Element

In Section 2, we conduct a literature review in two parts. First, we present relevant debates on different proposed drivers of social policy expansion, with existing work especially centering on pre–World War II Europe. We outline four mainstream arguments, which we later contrast with the argument made in this Element. The first alternative argument highlights elite support of social policy expansions due to economic motivations, notably demand for skilled workers or furthering international economic integration. The second argument centers on the role of reformist trade unions and social democratic parties. The third argument concerns changing international labor standards and norms, with international organizations playing an important role. The final argument, which is more closely related to ours, considers how elite concerns for resolving "the worker question" contributed to early welfare development to secure regime legitimacy.

The second literature pertains to elite perceptions of revolutionary threats, and how such perceptions drive political change, notably institutional changes pertaining to the electoral system, suffrage expansions, or broader democratization processes. These studies serve as a key building block for our argument. But we also highlight some critical differences and nuances, especially related to the notion of "credible commitments" to future redistribution, and the extent to which institutional change or (merely) adoption of policy programs is sufficient for such commitments.

In Section 3, we present our theoretical argument. We contend that different economic and political elites are often inherently reluctant to expand various rights and redistributive social policies that benefit poorer citizens or to open the political system to include new groups. Such policy and institutional changes come with notable costs, especially associated with increased tax burdens or loss of managerial control. Yet, elites may become consenters to "costly" social policies when they face a credible revolutionary threat to the political or economic system. Elites would rather consent to social policies and lose out monetarily from redistribution in its milder form (e.g., increased taxation and spending on social programs) than risk revolution and more extreme changes in power structure and redistribution (nationalization, collectivization, worker-controlled businesses, etc.).

In the first part of the section, we detail the factors that shape the objective probability of successful revolution or elites' subjective beliefs of what this probability is. We surmise that for a revolutionary threat to be credible, the relevant opposition groups must, *first*, have sufficient power resources to mount effective challenges and, *second*, have an ideological outlook compatible with revolutionary change. *Third*, elites must receive informative signals of both the capacity and intent of opposition groups to engage in revolutionary activities. In extension, we discuss how international linkages of domestic labor groups to the Comintern and the formation of worker and formation of soldier councils influenced all three factors, thereby making elites more susceptible to view a domestic revolutionary threat as credible.

In the second part, we discuss how elites respond to perceived credible revolutionary threats. Generally, elites may respond by pursuing repression or co-optation strategies. Political co-optation strategies include granting suffrage rights to previously excluded groups that constitute threats. Social co-optation strategies include granting greater access to material resources or leisure; for example, via working time regulation. We address how elites often resort to a combination of responses, but that the relative importance of these strategies hinges on the nature of the threat and other factors such as the presence of reformist and radial worker elements.

In Section 4, we present the in-depth case study of Norway, 1915–24. We detail how Norwegian elite groups – in the military, secret police, organized business, and the political establishment – sincerely feared that a worker-led revolution was imminent at different points in time during 1918–21. This threat was notably related to the transformation of the Labor party after the Bolshevik Revolution. With the strengthening of radical elements at the cost of reformists, the former even gained control over the Labor party and made it enter Comintern in 1919.

Responding to this perceived threat, heightened by local events such as strikes and soldier councils, elites planned or pursued a range of measures, often in a coordinated fashion, to avoid revolution. These measures included repressive policies, but, notably, also different political-institutional concessions and social policies. The goal of the latter measures seems to have been mitigating worker grievances and strengthening reformists in the unions and the Labor Party. We focus on how and why particular policies, which the elites had strongly resisted up until 1917, were adopted with little to no opposition. The most extensive discussion pertains to the adoption of the eight-hour workday. This was a long-sought-after goal by the workers, but one which both political and economic elites vehemently resisted until the revolutionary threat turned imminent. Other policies – not all of which were adopted – include socialization of means of production, worker participation in management, and old-age pensions. In addition, reforms were undertaken to preexisting policies and programs, including a massive expansion in subsidies to unemployment benefits and increased sickness and accident payments. Concerning institutional concessions, we consider the adoption of PR electoral rules and suffrage extensions. All these reforms were costly to the elites, either in pecuniary terms (through requiring increased taxes) or in the form of loss of political power.

In Section 5, we present the data collected for the cross-country analyses. First, we describe our new measures on labor regulation and social policies. Next, we present and discuss different proxies of revolutionary threat perceptions, focusing mostly on our main measures pertaining to invitations to and participation in Comintern.

Section 6 includes analyses that draw on these new measures and cover countries from across the world. We first test implications pertaining to work-time regulation using both cross-section and panel data and controlling for several, plausible alternative explanations. Some panel specifications include dual-fixed effects and country-specific time trends. And, while the treatment we are considering is not strictly exogenous, some of our tests approach a difference-in-differences logic, utilizing information from treated countries and nontreated ones, both before and after 1919. Countries facing an increased revolutionary threat, following Comintern invitations or erection of soldier and worker councils, on average limited working hours by substantially more in the succeeding years. These differences lingered on; states that experienced greater revolutionary threat in 1919 had lower working hours even at the end of the Cold War. We also consider alternative dependent variables and show that our main measure of revolutionary threat correlates with coverage of industrial workers in various redistributive welfare programs, including unemployment and sickness benefit programs, but also a general increase in coverage of different social groups.

In Section 7, we dig deeper into the question of why the policy effects from the Bolshevik shock persisted for so many decades. We outline different, plausible mechanisms, but focus on the foundation of new Communist parties in Comintern countries and present indicative evidence of this mechanism contributing to the persistent relationship.

In the conclusion, Section 8, we summarize our argument and main findings before discussing avenues for future research. Finally, we discuss how generalizable our findings are, and especially if they bear any relevance to later revolutionary periods with international repercussions such as the Cuban revolution of the 1950s.

2 Literature Review

2.1 Elites and Early Drivers of Social Policy Expansion

Our study is situated in the middle of the first period of welfare state expansion, extending from 1860 to World War II (Huber & Stephens, 2001). The welfare state literature has provided us with numerous theories explaining welfare state expansion in this era. We will focus on four central approaches that all make predictions pertaining to elite preferences for social policy. The first approach highlights elite acceptance, or even active support of social policy expansions because of economic motivations such as demand for skilled workers or easing international economic integration. We label this approach the *cross-class* perspective. The second approach highlights the role of reformist trade unions and social democratic parties, with their high mobilization capacity resulting in adoption of redistributive social measures. We label this the *class* perspective. The third approach considers the malleability of principles and norms for what elites believe is "right." Especially following major crises or the formation of transnational organizations, a norm cascade could result in encompassing social policy changes. We label this the *norm* perspective. Finally, we review arguments more closely related to ours addressing how elite concerns for "the worker question" and the popular legitimacy of regimes drove early welfare development. We label this the *worker question* perspective.

Before presenting the four approaches, we make an important conceptual clarification. We operate with a broad notion of "elites" in this Element (and clarify when we are speaking about more specific elite groups). By elites we mean groups of wealthy or politically powerful individuals with intrinsic interests in maintaining the current economic system (e.g., capitalism with private property) and existing political regime. Hence, elites typically encompass cabinet ministers and other leading figures in government parties, but also employers, capital owners, and landowners (and their various organizations). We do not assume that elites are unitary actors, but we do assume that different elite groups prefer the status quo over revolution and may therefore try to coordinate their policy responses to effectively mitigate revolutionary threats. In this regard, we note that actors can have "first-order" and "second-order" preferences, and that actors can switch between being antagonists, consenters, and protagonists for the same type of legislation depending on the context and perceived viable alternatives (Hacker & Pierson, 2002; Paster, 2013, 420). In some instances, strategic actors may push for the introduction of policies that they previously resisted, if they believe the policy averts a greater evil.

One strand of *cross-class theories* of welfare expansion focus on businesses interests, arguing that employers and their political representatives can have first-order preferences for welfare state development and labor regulation (see, e.g., Iversen, 2005; Iversen & Soskice, 2009; Mares, 2000, 2001, 2003; Martin & Swank, 2004; Skorge & Rasmussen, 2021; Soskice & Hall, 2001; Swank & Martin, 2001; Swenson, 1991a, 1991b, 1997, 2002, 2004). For instance, sectoral features related to exposure to international competition (Mares, 2005), firm size (Mares, 2003), or corporatist organizational structures (Martin & Swank, 2012) could induce some employers to support welfare policies.

The most prevalent such argument is the skill-supply argument (Estevez-Abe et al., 2001; Iversen & Soskice, 2019). Employers require employees to make risky investments in sector- or even firm-specific skills. By promoting social insurance, employees know that these investments will be compensated even if they should lose their job. This, in turn, increases the employee's willingness to invest in profitable, specific skills that employers require, inducing these groups to form pro-redistribution alliances. These cross-class coalitions shift the power balance in favor of welfare state development and inclusive political institutions that strengthen pro-welfare forces (Estevez-Abe et al., 2001; Iversen & Soskice, 2009, 2019). One empirical implication, which is relevant for our research context, is that we should observe clear elite splits along lines following skill dependencies, and countries or industries that require specialized skills should be more supportive of welfare policies.

Other cross-class perspectives highlight how exposure to international competition splits across class lines, with pro-redistributive coalitions forming among workers and employers in exposed sectors and anti-redistributive coalitions in sheltered domestic industries (Cameron, 1978; Mares, 2003, 2005). Workers and employers in exposed sectors are presumably supportive of redistribution since jobs are riskier, and, absent high wages (which reduces competitiveness and profits), social insurance is needed to compensate for the high risk of unemployment. Hence, we should observe clear elite splits along lines following dependency on international trade, and states with greater traded sectors should, all else equal, have more expansive welfare policies.

In contrast with the cross-class perspective, class theory, or power resource theory (Esping-Andersen, 1990; Korpi, 2006) arguments highlight the unique role played by reformist trade unions and social democratic parties. Their high mobilization capacity allows them to effectively push for redistributive social measures. In this perspective, employers are considered less exposed to the vagaries of life or labor market risks such as unemployment. Their access to capital also allows employers to effectively accumulate power resources. In contrast, workers have only their labor, which cannot be accumulated, and a high risk of unemployment, and they bear the burdens of income loss during sickness or old age. Given their inability to accumulate resources, workers must organize in trade unions and parties to effectively use their numerical strength to push through policies that would mitigate these risks. Developments that enhance the relative power of these organizations compared to employers should thus increase the likelihood of welfare state expansion. In the class perspective, elites are primarily antagonists to welfare state development, implying that they will consistently resist welfare state expansions, other redistributive policies, and changes challenging employers' managerial control.

The *norm* perspective highlights how norms and principles shape what policy is considered appropriate or "just" by elites and the public. As norms and principles change, elites come to promote new policies to solve what now is considered an unjust condition. This means welfare policy is carried out by consensus, with elites embracing policies that they previously resisted by adopting new principles for social justice. Studies of social learning and diffusion have identified how adoption of particular policies inspired similar policies in neighboring countries and how international organizations can diffuse both norms and rules and thus successfully promote new social standards (Brooks, 2004; Collier & Messick, 1975; Dobbin et al., 2007; Leisering, 2020; Schmitt et al., 2020; Schmitt et al., 2015; Weyland, 2005). In the social policy area, the ILO has historically been the most important organization in this regard. It was established in 1919, resulting from wartime bargains between states, big business, and organized labor, with the intent to homogenize labor standards across competing economies, blunt social unrest, and promote "social justice" (Schmitt et al., 2020; Schmitt et al., 2015; Strang & Chang, 1993, 240). Rasmussen (2021) finds that Versailles treaty signatories, and subsequently ILO members, were more likely to enact and implement eight-hour-day legislation, providing an alternative explanation of our outcomes of interest during the period under study, and we account for it in our case study and cross-country analysis. More generally, one relevant implication of the norm change perspective pertains to the wave-like spread of new policies and another is consensus around new social policy and elites viewing such policy as a legitimate end to promote "social justice."

The *worker question* perspective builds on the observation that industrialization and the growth of the industrial worker class lead to a legitimacy crisis for non-democratic regimes. With the advent of industrialization, and the rise of a new kind of worker not bound by the traditional obligations and constraints associated with work in agriculture, "the worker question" was formulated in nineteenth-century Europe. Elite representatives such as Napoleon III in France, Bismarck in Germany, Taafe in Austria, and Estrup in Denmark responded with different combinations of repressive and inclusionary policy initiatives intended as long-term strategies to co-opt workers and secure the regime's popular legitimacy (Luebbert, 1987; Therborn, 1984, 11–12). In this perspective, the primary movers are the elites, and specifically the conservative or liberal leaders of semi-democratic or autocratic regimes aiming to shore up support from workers (Therborn, 1984, 11–12). However, the perspective has not fully specified what factors are likely to trigger this need to shore up regime support, beyond broader considerations of socialist and worker threats.

Recently, scholars have generalized this perspective to include groups beyond industrial workers, highlighting how different autocratic regimes face potential challenges and require support from various social groups (e.g., Eibl, 2020; Knutsen & Rasmussen, 2018). Han (2021) shows how welfare-providing autocrats in Africa enjoy more popular support than other autocrats. Others have highlighted how preparing for and carrying out warfare, a vastly demanding project for the working and middle classes that strains regime legitimacy, push elites to pursue welfare policies even in nondemocratic settings (Obinger et al., 2018). In sum, elites, in certain contexts, may shift from being welfare policy antagonists to protagonists, in order to shore up legitimacy and ensure regime survival.

Our argument in Section 3 builds on and further develops the class and worker question arguments. Let us already here make a couple of specific points on how it differs from the reviewed perspectives.

First, our argument assumes that elites are inherently resistant to most forms of labor regulations or social policies due to redistributive costs and loss of managerial control, suggesting that elites often play the role of antagonists in policymaking. This runs counter to the cross-class perspective, where certain employers may prefer social insurance to make workers invest in cospecific skills. We note that employers in the relevant sectors can provide most forms of insurance through company- or sector-specific policies rather than broad national policies (Niihjuis, 2009). And, while broader national programs and policies may shift costs from employers to taxpayers, employers and other elite groups have other reasons to resist such policies. First, social programs raise labor costs either through increasing payroll taxes or by restricting normal work hours. Second, social regulation adversely affects labor supply by raising workers' reservation wages. For employers relying on skilled labor, the need to hire new workers to keep up production under reduced hours could lead to labor shortages in addition to higher wages. The skill argument, while applicable to preferences for generous social policies, is therefore harder to reconcile with a preference for stricter labor standards and reduced work hours, in particular. Third, policies such as labor standards constrain employers' managerial rights, circumscribing elites' ability to use their capital (Emmenegger, 2014). Fourth, in the historical period that we study, agriculture was still the most prominent sector in most economies (Broadberry et al., 2010). The most common employer was a landlord or farmer, who primarily viewed social policies of different kinds as a subsidy of urban interest (see, e.g., Rasmussen, 2021). We therefore find it plausible that elites, especially in the early twentieth century, often have an intrinsic interest in restraining expansive social policies.

Contrary to the class perspective, in which policy expansion takes place because of socialist parties, workers only indirectly cause policy change in our story; elites strategically respond to worker threats by taking up their demands and translating them into policies to avoid even worse scenarios. Also contrary to the class perspective, we stress that labor is not a monolith, but divided along ideological lines. Reformist parliamentarians stand against radical revolutionaries (Berman, 2006). This division was especially pertinent in the years following the Bolshevik Revolution.

The norm perspective also entails empirical implications that may be used to distinguish it from our argument, which we leverage in our empirical analyses.

Most importantly, insofar as the relevant norms are not prone to rapid reversals, it predicts that even proposed policies will stick and eventually be implemented. In contrast to fairness norms, revolutionary threat is transitory, suggesting that policies or policy proposals that may be changed without other costs will be abandoned once the revolutionary threat ebbs out.

As already noted, our argument resembles the worker question perspective. Yet, we elaborate on and contextualize this perspective by highlighting the immediate threat associated with the *bifurcation* of domestic labor movements and their *international linkages* (through Comintern). We also elaborate on the conditions under which elites come to believe a revolutionary threat is credible, and how this can incentivize elites to pursue different combinations of repressive and inclusionary strategies.

2.2 Revolutionary Threats and Political Change

In this section, we review theories and studies that address our main independent variable, namely elites' perceptions of revolutionary threat, and how this may drive political change. Arguments on the role of revolutionary threat have mainly centered on political-institutional changes pertaining to suffrage extensions to previously disenfranchised groups, notably the working classes, or democratization processes more generally. Several empirical studies also speak to how mass collective action and enhanced threats of forced regime change may drive political elites to concede political (and other) changes that they may not originally want, but ultimately accept in order to stave off the even worse prospect of a revolution. Finally, we focus on the notion of "credible commitments" to future redistribution, and how certain such concessions by elites may mitigate revolutionary threats. We address how credible commitments can be made by implementing certain social policy programs, even absent political-institutional changes, as these programs create different lock-in effects.

A core assumption of our theoretical argument is that incumbent political elites make different concessions to nonelite groups when the latter can credibly threaten a revolution that would upend the political system and hurt the economic interests of the elites. Concession, be it in the form of franchise expansions or costly redistributive economic policies, is not something self-interested elites initially desire or hand out easily. Yet, they can still be willing to entertain the option if it helps mitigate the revolutionary threat; such concessions are perceived a preferable "lesser evil" (Djuve et al., 2020) when the status quo is no longer tenable.

This lesser-evil notion is central to prominent theories of democratization (see also, e.g., Acemoglu & Robinson, 2000; Boix & Stokes, 2003), and discussed explicitly in Acemoglu and Robinson (2006), in whose core theoretical model both elites and citizens are motivated by consumption, but instrumentally care about the political regime since it influences who wields political power, and thus who sets redistributive policy. Elites want to retain autocracy and keep taxation and redistributive spending low, whereas citizens prefer democracy with extensive suffrage, where they can control economic policy. Thus, elites will maintain autocracy and keep a lid on redistributive policies during normal times. However, when a credible threat of revolution arises – for example, due to an economic crisis, revolutionary fervor in neighboring countries spilling over, or citizens for some other reason overcoming their collective action problems – incumbent elites will try to preempt it by extending suffrage to the citizens threatening revolution. Simply promising redistribution under the same autocratic system may not help stave off revolution; such promises are not credible and quickly disregarded once the revolutionary threat dissipates.

The expectation that revolutionary threat leads to suffrage extensions, and democratization more generally, is supported by different pieces of evidence. Przeworski (2009) finds that strikes, riots, and demonstrations precede franchise extensions, particularly class-based extensions. Pertinent to our argument, Aidt and Jensen (2014) highlight how the international situation, and especially diffusion of information from revolutionary and other relevant events abroad, enhances revolutionary threat domestically (see also, Weyland, 2014, 2019). This, in turn, relates to franchise extensions in a panel of European countries in the nineteenth and early twentieth centuries. The international dimension of regime change, and how democratization processes cluster temporally due to features of the international political system, major global shocks, or cross-border learning, is also well documented by the broader literature on "democratization waves" (Huntington, 1991; Markoff & White, 2009).

Indeed, popular revolutions come in temporal waves, globally, with peaks coming in 1848 and at the end of World War I (Djuve et al., 2020; Weyland, 2014). In several detailed studies that address the international dimension of revolutionary threat perceptions, Weyland (2014, 2019) provides credible evidence on cross-border spillover. He highlights the role of informational cues and cognitive-psychological heuristics when detailing the mechanisms through which prospective revolutionaries – often unsuccessfully (and especially so in early modern history) – were triggered by particularly vivid and noticeable revolutionary events such as France 1848 and Russia 1917.

Other studies have shown how the mobilization of sustained opposition campaigns, more generally, induce subsequent democratization, especially when opposition campaigns employ nonviolent tactics and attract numerous protesters (e.g., Celestino & Gleditsch, 2013; Chenoweth & Belgioioso, 2019;

Chenoweth & Stephan, 2011). Interestingly for our study, Dahlum et al. (2019) find that opposition campaigns are especially likely to engender democratization when they are dominated by urban industrial workers. This social group has a comparatively high capacity for organizing effective collective action, drawing on organizational resources in the form of unions and left-wing parties, international networks, and inspiring ideologies (see, e.g., Collier, 1999; Rueschemeyer et al., 1992).

Part of the correlation between mass mobilization and democratization is explained by sustained mass protests leading to outright revolution in some cases. However, and following Acemoglu and Robinson's theoretical argument, a much larger portion of democratization processes are so-called incumbent-guided liberalization episodes (Djuve et al., 2020), where autocratic elites (alone or in negotiations with opposition actors) liberalize the regime when facing threatening mass protests. When protesters amass in the streets and threaten the regime with a revolution, elites grant suffrage extensions, electoral rule changes (see Ahmed, 2012), or other democratic concessions to mitigate the threat.

Counter to Acemoglu and Robinson (2006), our theoretical argument assumes that regime change and franchise expansion are not necessary requisites for credible guarantees of future redistribution to the lower classes (though they may certainly help). Knutsen and Rasmussen (2018) highlight that the legislation of new social programs creates lock-in effects that tie elites to these programs once initiated. First, there are substantial sunk costs with starting up such programs; once implemented and operative, it is relatively less expensive to continue the program (and thus less rewarding for elites to walk it back, compared to never implementing it). Second, discontinuing a popular program creates a clear focal point on which opponents may organize effective, large-scale opposition against the regime. This is likely one reason why large-scale social policy programs are seldom discontinued (Knutsen & Rasmussen, 2018), and when substantial cutbacks in spending happen, mass collective action frequently arises (Ponticelli & Voth, 2020).

Empirically, Knutsen and Rasmussen (2018) show how even autocratic regimes may construct old-age pension programs to funnel resources to particular social groups to placate them and ensure regime survival. This follows a large literature on autocratic politics highlighting how "co-optation" of critical groups through economic policies, alongside repression, is one of the major strategies used to prolong regime survival (e.g., Gerschewski, 2013; Miller, 2015; Wintrobe, 1998; see also the literature on the worker question reviewed earlier).

If true, the assumption of credible future redistribution via social policy programs means that implementing such programs could be used to mitigate revolutionary threats posed by, say, industrial workers, insofar as grievances are (at least partly) driven by economic concerns. In contrast, mere promises of discretionary redistribution, or even promises of future policy programs, should not be considered as credible guarantees.

3 A Theory of Elites' Policy Responses to Revolutionary Threats

The argument that we advance centers on different economic and political elites being reluctant to give policy concessions or open up the political system to new groups, as this brings costs, notably associated with increased taxes, reduced revenues, and reduced political influence. Yet, elites may become consenters to "costly" social policies when they face a credible revolutionary threat and try to avoid a revolution (accompanied by even more costly policies). Similarly, elites may take the political cost (loss in parliamentary seats) incurred by, say, adopting new electoral rules if this means preventing revolution. We surmise that there are different nonrationalist (cognitive heuristics) as well as rational mechanisms that may fuel elite fear of revolution in certain situations. We further elaborate on elites' options to use political inclusion exclusively or in tandem with social policy concessions, as well as how these "carrots" may be combined with different "sticks" in the form of repression, to mitigate revolutionary threats. We will anchor this argument in a particular historical context.

The Russian Revolution of 1917 eventually brought the Bolsheviks to power, introducing a Communist state that would shake up the international system. The Bolsheviks saw their revolution as a prelude to World Revolution (Pons, 2014, 15), and even considered revolutions abroad as key to their own long-term regime survival (Carr, 1979, 12–13; Pons, 2014, 8–9). Comintern was established to guide revolutionary groups outside Russia (McDermott & Agnew, 1996). It was de facto controlled by the Russian Communist Party's Politburo, and worked alongside the Russian Ministry of Foreign Affairs (Pons, 2014, 12). Comintern's mission, in Trotsky's (1919) words, was to bring together the world's true revolutionaries, eschewing the "social-traitor parties." It established local branches to spread propaganda, and later required that all member parties adhere to Lenin's twenty-one points from the second conference, including that capitalist societies had progressed to a state of "civil war" (Sundvall, 2017). Comintern also provided extensive funding for aspiring communist parties (McDermott & Agnew, 1996).

Carr (1979, 13) notes that, for a while, "the hope of a world revolution seemed to materialize." Worker- and soldier councils, strikes, and uprisings surged in many countries. Still, hopes of worldwide revolution were short-lived. No durable communist regime outside Russia materialized. In 1921, Lenin admitted that the revolutionary trajectory had "not been as linear as we had expected."

Why was the Bolshevik Revolution not followed by similar successful revolutions elsewhere? Even if it did not result in successful revolutions, did it lead to major political and policy changes outside Russia? One resolution to answering both questions lies in recognizing that while the revolution was a symbol for labor and revolutionaries globally, it also inspired counterstrategies by economic and political elites. Fearing revolution, elites responded with several political and economic reforms, aiming to appease and create vested interests among (parts of) the labor movements. In the next section, we outline a more general argument on why and how elites respond to credible revolutionary threats by strategically providing policy concessions.

3.1 Elite Preferences, Power Resources, and Information Signals

In this section, we outline the different building blocks of our argument, detailing the factors that shape the objective probability of successful revolution or elites' subjective beliefs in this probability. In brief, we contend that for a revolutionary threat to be credible, the relevant opposition groups must (1) have sufficient power resources to mount effective challenges, and (2) espouse preferences for revolutionary change, for instance, by adhering to an ideology of radical societal transformation. Finally, (3) elites must receive informative signals of both (a) the capacity and (b) the intent of opposition groups to engage in revolutionary activities, which they must subsequently interpret. In extension, we discuss how certain international linkages (of domestic labor groups to the Comintern specifically) influence all three factors, making elites more susceptible to view a revolutionary threat as credible.

The underlying question that our theoretical argument addresses is as follows: Why would economic and political elites accept extensive social policy arrangements that (often) redistribute resources or control to relatively disadvantaged citizens? We argue that elites may become consenters to social policies when they face a credible revolutionary threat to the political and/or economic system. In this situation, accepting costly social policies may be the "lesser evil" if it helps reduce the revolutionary threat. Elites would rather consent to social policies and lose out monetarily from redistribution in its milder form (e.g., increased taxation and spending on social programs) than risk revolution and more extreme changes in power structure *and* redistribution (nationalization, collectivization, etc.).[5] This also holds for labor standards.

---

[5] Threats of strikes, riots, and other forms of instability may also be costly to both political and economic elites, though far less so than a revolution, and might thus, in certain instances, also incentivize policy concessions from the elites. Yet, such "milder forms" of collective action may be especially influential through increasing the perceived risk of a subsequent revolution. Revolutions seldom start in a vacuum, but are often triggered by strikes, riots, and initially

It is presumably better to accept some government encroachment on employers' rights to manage their workers through work-hour regulations and safety protections, than having firms placed under worker control.

This argument follows key rationalist contributions to the democratization literature reviewed in Section 2.2 (e.g., Acemoglu & Robinson, 2006; Aidt & Jensen, 2014; Boix, 2003) in highlighting that elites may provide concessions to the lower classes to avoid revolution. In these works, concessions come in the form of political liberalization and suffrage expansions, which shift political power to the lower classes, thereby ensuring worker influence. Yet, and counter to Acemoglu and Robinson (2006), we highlight that regime change and franchise expansion may be helpful, but are not necessary requisites for credible guarantees of future redistribution. Instead, we follow Knutsen and Rasmussen (2018), who highlight that implementing new social programs, and other major policy initiatives, creates lock-in effects and serves to tie elites to these programs once initiated. As discussed in Section 2.2, such programs entail sunk costs (investment in monitoring capacity, complementary human capital investments, infrastructure, hiring new workers, etc.) that create lock-in effects once investments are made and they create clear *focal points* on which opponents of the regime/policy change may organize effective, large-scale opposition. Therefore, social policy programs, once implemented, generate credible guarantees of future redistribution to its recipients. In contrast, mere promises of future policy initiatives lack these features, and are therefore often noncredible (as detailed and illustrated by our case study of Norway in Section 4).

Insofar as *credible* revolutionary threats drive elites to provide social policy concessions, a key question for understanding welfare state expansion is what factors shape elites' perceptions of the likelihood of revolution? Specifically, we outline three factors that shape the objective probability of successful revolution *and* elites' estimates of this probability, which may be influenced by more rational calculations as well as several cognitive heuristics.

First, opposition groups must possess power resources to be a viable threat. Occupying key sectors of the economy and being able to inflict economic costs on political adversaries if needed (for instance via crippling mass strikes) is important in this regard. Moreover, for urban workers, key resources have historically resided in hierarchical and effective organizations that enable them to solve collective action problems and mobilize large numbers, including trade unions, councils, and party organizations. This helps explain why anti-regime mass opposition mobilized by urban workers is relatively effective in

---

minor forms of disorder, which snowball into even larger mass collective action and eventually trigger a revolution (e.g., Kuran, 1989; Weyland, 2019).

achieving their goals (e.g., Dahlum et al., 2019). International linkages are another key factor. Such linkages may provide monetary resources and organizational know-how, even for smaller groups. Notably, our empirical analysis highlights how Comintern advanced domestic organizational structures, including new Communist parties, empowering potential left-wing revolutionaries.

Second, it must be clear that the group is *motivated* to undertake revolutionary actions. For revolutionary threats to be credible, opposition groups must view revolution as legitimate, aspiring to an ideology of radical societal transformation; for instance, aiming to transform the economy's ownership structure by socializing property. Certain ideologies explicitly consider revolution as one of several legitimate strategies, or even the only effective and legitimate course of action: Pursuing legislative change through parliament may explicitly be rejected, with movements instead spurring extra-parliamentary action such as strikes or mass protests, even considering violent means as necessary. Historically, this description fits to parties and unions adhering to Communism, as opposed to the reformism of social democrats (Lipset, 1983). We detail and illustrate the revolutionary ideology of parts of the early-twentieth-century labor movement in the empirical sections.

Third, elites must receive some sort of informative signal, that is, some indication of the resources and motives of opposition groups, which they must subsequently interpret (Fearon, 1995; Vis, 2019; Weyland, 2019). Our argument does not work if elites – be it correctly or mistakenly – assume that opposition groups are unwilling or unable to undertake a revolution.

The nature and interpretation of information signals shape elites' perceptions of credibility of revolutionary threats. Sometimes revolutionary movements may send strong and clear signals on their motivations and resources. In other contexts, such signaling is difficult. Certain reformist labor unions or parties unwilling to engage in revolutionary activities might have incentives to "bluff," and pose as revolutionary, to obtain concessions. Thus, elites can have a hard time distinguishing revolutionaries from reformists.

Elites' capacity to absorb signals, and how they go about interpreting them, are also relevant factors. While some elite actors may decipher information about the motivation and capacity of opposition groups and update beliefs in a relatively unbiased and "rational" manner, others make decisions under uncertainty and time pressure, resorting to various cognitive shortcuts (Vis, 2019; for applications to revolutionary threats, see Weyland 2014, 2019). Revolutions are complex and relatively rare events, making it even harder for elite actors to analyze prospects of revolutions without relying on cognitive heuristics. Bluntly assuming that the future will reflect the past, elites might evaluate ongoing processes by searching for patterns and analogous events found in past revolutionary settings (Aidt & Jensen, 2014), for which the Bolshevik Revolution long remained a primary reference point (Hobsbawm, 1994). Elites may be "aided" in making these shortcuts, as newspapers or other media readily report front-page news on revolutions abroad. Further, given the so-called availability heuristic (Vis, 2019), elites, as other people, may inadvertently focus on large and salient events, thus overestimating the baseline probability of revolution (as may prospective revolutionaries; see Weyland, 2014). Since big historical events create symbols that work as cognitive maps to understand current events, the Bolshevik Revolution likely formed many elites' perceptions of domestic conditions and the capacities and motivations of national left-wing groups (and perhaps more so than revolutionary events even in neighboring countries; c.f., Aidt and Jensen, 2014).

Hence, international or domestic factors and events that enhance the power resources of potential revolutionaries, pull their ideology in a revolutionary direction, or provide information signals to elites about the capabilities and revolutionary intent of opposition groups, enhance the perceived credibility of revolutionary threats. Importantly for our research context, ties with the Russian revolutionary regime, especially Comintern membership from 1919, may have enhanced all three above-discussed aspects. First, Comintern often provided material resources directly to relevant movements and helped the founding of new Communist parties, thus enhancing organizational capacity. Second, the related international network and exchanges presumably diffused revolutionary ideology. Third, Comintern membership served as a strong signal to elites, increasing perceptions of a domestic revolution being likely.[6]

3.2 Elite Responses

In this section, we discuss the process by which elites decide how to respond when facing (perceived) revolutionary threats. Generally, elites may respond by pursuing either repression or co-optation strategies, or a combination. Our theoretical argument and analyses mainly focus on co-optation but we first briefly discuss repression strategies.

While repression is typically recognized as a key strategy of autocratic elites (Gerschewski, 2013; Wintrobe, 1998), all types of regimes repress (although democracies often opt for softer types of repression and, generally, repress less; Davenport (2007). Repression could effectively mitigate revolutionary threats

---

[6] The formation of worker and soldier councils following the Zimmerwald declaration played a similar role. Domestic worker councils with perceived linkages to an international revolutionary movement, espousing radical ideology, posed a potential revolutionary threat. The formation of soldier councils may have been an even stronger signal of the revolutionary threat posed by domestic groups.

due to several mechanisms, for instance, because it instills fear in potential participants in anti-regime collective action and thus reduces willingness to participate (Young, 2019). Repression can be particularly effective and relatively costless when targeted at early efforts at mobilization, before they cascade into mass uprisings (Sullivan, 2016) or when targeting particularly influential opposition "activists" (Demirel-Pegg & Rasler, 2021). Yet, repression – and especially violent and visible repression that increases anti-regime grievances and may serve as focal points for further mobilization – has the potential of creating "backlash" (e.g., Carey, 2006; Sullivan & Davenport, 2017). Violent repression sometimes also creates frictions and possible defection within the security apparatus and, more widely, among elites, which is particularly dangerous for the regime (e.g., Bellin, 2012; Nepstad, 2013). Hence, governments facing revolutionary threats may think carefully through when, whom, or how to repress, but also whether repression should be complemented, or even entirely substituted with, co-optation strategies, even when such strategies are costly.

When facing (perceived) revolutionary threats, elites thus often choose to respond mainly by pursuing co-optation strategies. Co-optation directed towards larger social groups can come in at least two forms, political and economic inclusion. Political inclusion contains granting participation rights to previously excluded groups. Economic inclusion entails granting greater access to material resources.

Both strategies aim at defusing revolutionary threats by increasing the legitimacy of the current system and mitigating core grievances within key opposition segments via inclusion. We mainly focus on economic inclusion through social policies and labor regulations, but also consider political inclusion. Political inclusion is especially viable if it can help elites to split opposition groups (e.g., by co-opting moderates and weakening revolutionaries). This (at least latent) fault line was present in worker movements in many countries following the Bolshevik Revolution, with revolutionary radicals of various sorts standing against reformist-oriented social democrats. The ideological struggle between these groups originated in their differing perceptions of the viability of a parliamentary, reformist strategy as a road to social transformation of society (Berman, 2006). The relative size and influence of these groups within the worker movement were arguably contingent on different factors, including institutional ones. Notably, in countries were electoral systems disfavored worker parties, resulting in under-representation in parliament, reformists faced an uphill battle against radicals promoting extra-parliamentary action as the most effective strategy for achieving policy ends. One implication of this insight is that elites could contribute to strengthening the relative position of the reformists through pursuing electoral rule reform that increased the electoral pay-offs for social democrats.

More generally, as highlighted by Acemoglu & Robinson (2006), providing political rights and reforming institutions to enhance the political power of opposition groups are key strategies for mitigating revolutionary threats. Down the road, such expansions of political rights may also induce politicians to adopt more expansive social policy programs to cater to the recently empowered groups, thus suggesting one additional long-term mechanism (see Section 7) through which revolutionary threat may affect social policy outcomes of interest in this Element.

However, we contend that elites can credibly respond to revolutionary threats also when stopping short of extending political rights, instead co-opting threats by implementing reforms and changing various policies in directions desired by the potential revolutionaries. The group that constituted the primary threat to elites – especially in industrializing or industrialized countries – in the period that we study was urban workers, often organized in labor unions, councils, and socialist parties. Hence, policies introduced to stem revolutionary threats should primarily target this group. Prime examples are social policies with a redistributive component that encompass workers, and notably programs that guard against major work and life risks such as unemployment, sickness, and old age. We will discuss and test the relationship between revolutionary threat and such social policy programs in our empirical analysis. One empirical implication of our argument is that when perceptions of revolutionary threats are enhanced, governments are more likely to expand such social policy programs to cover urban workers.

Yet, the perhaps most important demand made by close to all labor organizations within our research context was the eight-hour day/forty-eight-hour week. This demand was made already by the First Socialist International in the 1860s, but elites around the world resisted. Employers typically rejected any form of working time regulation and international conventions only regulated the fringes of the issue area (night work). In Norway, the worker commission of 1885 made a formal proposal for the eight-hour day, but no legislative action was taken, with employers resisting because it encroached on their managerial powers and threatened profits.

Indicatively, the eight-hour day was one of the first key changes made by the Bolsheviks in Russia in November 1917, setting a concrete standard for labor movements where revolution had not (yet) taken hold. If employers and governments wanted to co-opt labor to avoid revolution, the eight-hour day was a prime tool. Hence, regulations on working time pertaining to industrial workers is our main outcome of interest in the qualitative case study on Norway and the cross-national analysis. A central empirical implication of our argument is that when perceptions of revolutionary threats are enhanced, elite groups are more likely to promote legislation that reduces the number of working hours for industrial workers.

Before turning to our case study, we discuss one caveat: Our argument builds on the assumption that elites share a preference for securing their long-term survival in power and the continuation of the current political-economic order. However, elites are not all the same, and in our case study we, for example, distinguish between different political elites, military elites, and business owners. Inevitably, there will be heterogeneity in both the preferences and threat perceptions between (and within) such groups. We surmise that the heterogeneity in preferences and awareness to different threats originate primarily in where they derive their resources from. For example, political elites should be more concerned by threats to the political system, and thus their powerbase, but be more open to bargain away parts of the managerial prerogatives in the business sector. Similarly, employers should be more open about allowing extensions of political rights, especially if they perceive that such extensions can credibly protect their managerial powers in the long term. Elites might thus come under cross-pressure from different economic and political considerations. This increases coordination problems, with individual elite members taking different positions depending on individual cost–benefit analyses.

Nonetheless, elite strength depends on unity, and the perceived revolutionary threat after the Bolshevik Revolution pertained simultaneously to the political regime and the economic system. Furthermore, the leading politicians of the day were often also captains of industry, landlords, or shipowners. Gunnar Knudsen, the main political figure in Norway between 1905 and 1920 was all four: factory owner, landlord, merchant, and politician. Elite intermingling across subgroups was common. Hence, there were strong incentives and possibilities for different elite groups to coordinate their responses, and our historical case study of Norway illustrates that they (mostly) were able to do so.

4 Case Study: Revolutionary Fear and Elite Responses in Norway, 1915–24

For our case study of social policy development in early-twentieth-century Norway, we draw on numerous sources, including work by historians. We detail how various elite members thought that revolution was imminent between 1918 and 1921 and how they, often in a coordinated fashion, responded by pursuing a complex sticks-and-carrots strategy to avoid a revolution. Regarding the carrots, we focus on the eight-hour day, but also discuss the trajectory and timing of policymaking and institutional reforms in several other areas, including electoral rules, collective agreements, and old-age pensions. These changes were pursued with the aim of mitigating worker grievances and strengthening the reformist part of the labor movement (Bjørnson, 1990; Danielsen, 1984; Fure, 1983; Knutsen, 1994, 43–46). In brief, we document how:

- Labor, as represented by core actors in the Labor Party and several unions, underwent a dramatic change following the Bolshevik Revolution, with radical elements strengthened at the cost of reformists.
- Elites came to believe that revolution was possible and imminent. This change in beliefs was directly tied to foreign revolutionary events in tandem with domestic developments, notably Comintern membership of the Labor party and the adoption of radical ideology in much of the worker movement.
- Elites responded by various measures aimed at "incorporating" the labor movement politically through electoral reforms and economically through various social policy reforms.
- These policies had previously been opposed by the elites (indeed, the very same politicians).
- Measures introduced during the period of high revolutionary threat tended to stick, whereas proposals that had yet to be implemented before the threat subsided, after 1921, were shelved.

Concerning the economic elites, we mainly consider the Norwegian Employer Association (Norsk Arbeidsgiver Forening, NAF), the leading employer organization from 1900 (Knutsen, 1994). We consider the political elites as being constituted by the residing governments (Gunnar Knudsen Liberal Party [Venstre] PM 1913–20 and Otto B. Halvorsen Conservative Party [Høyre] PM 1920–21), Conservative and Liberal Party MPs, and their party organizations.[7] In the state apparatus, we focus on the defense intelligence office (Generalstabens Efterretningkontor), secret police (Oppdagelsespolitiet), military high command (Generalstaben), and provisory security commission. The labor movement is regarded as (composed by) the Labor Party (Det Norske Arbeiderparti, DnA), the Trade Union Federation (Arbeidernes Faglige Landsorganisasjon, AFL), the Labor Party's youth wing (Norges socialdemokratiske Ungdomsforbund, NU), and the short-lived worker and soldier council movement. Hence, we cover the principal organizations and arenas for coordination and decision making in Norway.

---

[7] Party archives are – unfortunately – missing for our period. The Nazi occupation in 1940 led to this loss, and the archives have never been recovered. Historians have since then used various alternatives sources such as diaries to reconstruct preferences and political considerations (e.g, Danielsen, 1984). We have corresponded with several leading historians (e.g., N. Agøy, N. Brandal, Å. Egge, F. Olstad) on this period to ensure that we have consulted the most relevant material.

4.1 Norwegian Labor Goes Revolutionary

We here document how the labor movement in Norway split into reformists and radicals. The former aimed to achieve social change through parliament (the Storting), whereas the latter wanted to pursue a strategy of extra-parliamentarian action. We show how the radicals, following the Bolshevik Revolution, took control over the main party organization and made the Labor Party a Comintern member. Later, a process of "moderation" was fostered by the various reforms and inclusive policies pursued by the elites, including the eight-hour workday law and electoral system reform. These efforts strengthened the moderate reformists at the cost of the radicals.

The Norwegian Labor Party (DnA), founded in 1887, was inspired by Marxist thinking from its inception. The first party program stated that DnA "endeavors to hand over the means of production to social common property and change production from capitalist to socialist" (DnA, 1918). Such ideas were slowly abandoned as reformism became the leading principle before the turn of century, acknowledging the importance of achieving social change through legislation in parliament. The trade union federation (AFL), founded at DnA's behest in 1899, was a means to achieve changes in wage and working conditions through bargaining with employers. Thus DnA and AFL were bound at the hip and dual membership was practiced. The unions and party coordinated their demands against employers and politicians.

In early 1917, reformist leaders such as Olaf Lian held leadership positions in both DnA and AFL. Radical elements were in a minority, largely originating from Fagoposisjonen of 1911 – a syndicalist movement within AFL – and the youth organization. Fagoposisjonen argued for sabotage, boycott, and sympathy strikes as legitimate weapons against employers (Olstad, 1998, 173). Its leader, Martin Tranmæl, wanted to radicalize the union movement "to make it ready for revolutionary mass-action" (Bjørgum, 2017, 45). He wrote the group's ideological program of 1913, stating that "improvements cannot only take place within the established frame of capitalism, but one must also work to destroy [capitalism] and introduce the socialist social order" (Tranmæl, 1913, 5).

The 1917 revolution strengthened the radical movement, especially in DnA.[8] Following the March revolution, Tranmæl demanded that workers organize

---

[8] Historians debate exactly how radical Norwegian social democrats were, or what was meant by "revolutionary mass-action." The seminal study by Fure (1983) argues that there is clear evidence of planning for armed rebellion in November 1918. Sørensen & Brandal (2018) argue that while social democrats pursued a polarizing and extremist rhetoric, they remained committed to democracy (see also Bjørnson, 1990, 547). In this reading, the Norwegian social democrats only continued a long tradition of civil society organization within the bounds of the political regime. We note that our theoretical argument is not dependent on whether the social democrats were planning revolution. Instead, our argument hinges on elites believing the DnA was revolutionary. The only historical study

a general strike against the war, and arm themselves against the coming counterrevolutionary attempts by the bourgeoisie. For Tranmæl, the revolution in March 1917 heralded "the fall of class-society and the introduction of socialism . . . one can now clearly see that the fire will spread with a strength such that it cannot be stopped" (Bjørgum, 2017, 44–45). Still, Tranmæl's attempts at bringing down the reformist leadership of DnA and union congress were outmaneuvered by the reformists.

The November Revolution would decisively tip the power balance towards the radicals within DnA (Fure, 1983; Sundvall, 2017). The news from Russia led to major organizational and ideological transformations almost immediately. The labor paper, *Klassekampen* published the Zimmerwald declaration, urging sympathizers to "establish everywhere soldier and worker councils as your body in the struggle for peace!" (Bjørnson, 1990, 509). Radicals would establish and coordinate worker- and soldier councils around the country, offering Tranmæl a base of support outside the established frameworks of DnA and AFL. Among the resolutions adopted at the worker councils' national conference on March 24, 1918, was the immediate introduction of the eight-hour day and, if the government ignored their demands, "political mass-strikes" (Bjørnson, 1990, 516–517).

By 1918, the radicals had grown strong enough to challenge the reformists. Their recommendation to the national party meeting in March stated that "as a revolutionary class party, [DnA] cannot recognize the affluent classes' right to economic exploitation and repression of the working class even if this exploitation and repression is supported by a majority in parliament. [DNA] must therefore reserve the right to use revolutionary mass-action in the fight for the economic liberation of the working-class" (DnA, 1918).

The position of the revolutionaries, also those with syndicalist orientation, was thus to push the party towards extra-parliamentary action, away from reformism and parliamentarianism. Ole O. Lian, party vice-chairman in 1918, argued against this belief that a "revolutionary coup" was possible in Norway; the only viable option for influence was to secure majority support in the population.[9] Tranmæl countered that "the majority confuses parliamentarianism with popular rule. One has a superstitious belief in parliamentarianism. Such a superstitious belief will lead to a weakening of worker power and to

---

indicating this was not so, by Hobson and Kristiansen (2001, 169), has been criticized for not using the available source material (Agøy, 2002). Moreover, even these authors argue that the military command decisively changed their understanding of the revolutionary threat in 1917, and that local agitation came to be an expression of social radicalism.

[9] Specifically, Lian ruled out any general strikes aimed at parliament since all food supplies were controlled by municipal administration and the state. The only possible outcome from the mass-revolutionary action that the radicals wanted, Lian argued, would be to "knock our own feet from under ourselves" (Bjørnson, 1990, 531; DnA, 1918, 35–40)

nothing but great disappointments" (DnA, 1918, 41). The radical Eugene Olaussen added that "we cannot achieve electoral majority with the current electoral system, and the bourgeoisie knows this. Therefore, they will resist a just electoral system, if necessary, with arms" (DnA, 1918, 61–62.).

The reformists lost at the 1918 meeting, and the radicals gained majority. Tranmæl became party secretary, with all reformists relinquishing their positions in the party leadership.

In November 1918, following the German revolution, the new party leadership believed a revolution in Norway was possible, and several members started working on (subsequently abandoned) plans on "arrangements for a quick takeover of power" (Fure, 1983, 473). Planning group notes show that a takeover would be facilitated by the massive organization of worker councils, and the immediate reforms to be implemented were socialization of means of production and the eight-hour day. Tranmæl was designated to be "leader of the revolution" (Fure, 1983, 473–476).

How far did the radicals go in preparing for revolutionary action? According to reports found in the secret police archives, they included the gathering of arms. A member among the DnA leadership reportedly told an "Entente agent" that "weapons and ammunition were assembled on various places. . .. When action was to be taken, workers would be well armed."[10] Still, historians estimate that any weapons the movement possessed were very limited (Agøy, 1994). Regardless, the German revolution had strengthened the position of the syndicalists also in AFL. This worsened the position of the reformists, who had seen the federation as their bastion against DnA's radicalism (Fure, 1983, 65).

In 1919, DnA became further radicalized when its national convention even encouraged MPs to strike and soldier councils to be formed and prepare for mobilization (DnA, 1919, 12). It considered Norway to be in a "state of maturation for the revolution and socialism."[11] The envisioned society was one where voting rights were to be denied those "that live on the exploitation of others' labor," and this "socialist society must organizationally be built on worker-, farmer- and fisherman-councils" (DnA, 1919, 15). More generally, parliamentary means to policy change were now eschewed for a postrevolutionary socialist society (Fure, 1983, 92–93).

In addition, DnA also underwent organizational changes and shifted tactics. For instance, the role of the soldier councils was expanded from a defensive

---

[10] (Generalstabens etteretningskontor til sjefen for justisdepartementet 28.11.1918. Den revolusjonære bevegelse i Norge i 1918.) The seminal historian on DnA in this period (Fure, 1983, 479), advises some restraint in interpreting this statement as the fellow in question was known to exaggerate.

[11] DnA Landsmøteprotokoll, 1919, 12. Social-demokraten, May 8, 1919.

measure to an offensive strategy to "dismantle the military" (DnA, 1919, 44). Notably, the party decided to join Comintern, and the decision was front-page news in conservative and liberal newspapers.

Comintern membership was highly contentious within DnA. Already in 1919, the social democrats formed their own parliamentary group. With the election of 1921 (under the new PR rules, which significantly reduced the disproportionality of the system), they broke out and established the "Norwegian Social Democratic Party," achieving 9.2 percent of the vote, whereas DnA achieved 21.3 percent, about similar to what the (unified) party achieved in 1918. The reformists would rejoin DnA in 1927.

Vice-chairman Emil Stang was the single delegate representing DnA at Comintern's First Congress in 1919, and the party joined in late 1919. At the second conference, DnA had one of the largest delegations: Ten delegates arrived in Moscow, including the youth organization leader (and future PM) Einar Gerhardsen.

It is important to recognize the revolutionary nature of the Comintern. Its aim, as recognized by Lenin's twenty-one theses, presented by Comintern's leader Zinonev at the second conference, was to establish organizations that could function as unit in the European "civil war." The organization were to be divided into isolated cells that could operate independently of each other, but following a hierarchal system; the goal was to create communist parties that could survive the coming world revolution (Sundvall, 2017). Adhering to the Comintern theses also meant the expulsion of "reformist traitors" to avoid the "danger of being watered down by elements characterized by vacillation and half-measures."[12] House clearing was mandatory, and so was engaging in illegal activities. These organizational changes were deemed necessary because "the Communist Party should be the vanguard, the front-line troops of the proletariat, leading in all phases of its revolutionary class struggle and the subsequent transitional period toward the realization of socialism."[13]

DnA took an active role in both legal and illegal work within Comintern. Illegal transportation of Soviet propaganda and couriers was organized by a secret committee in Kristiania (the pre-1925 name for Oslo), and party offices were used to hide illegals traveling to and from Russia (Fure, 1983, 468–471). A German spy report also outlines that Norway was used as a station to transport funds to practically the whole world (Fure, 1983). Prominent DnA members participated in the smuggling. Einar Gerhardsen, for example, smuggled emeralds

---

[12] www.marxists.org/history/international/comintern/2nd-congress/ch07.htm.
[13] www.marxists.org/history/international/comintern/2nd-congress/ch07.htm.

hidden in toothpaste tubes after the Comintern meeting of 1920. Another DnA member was stopped with fifty-one gold bars in his luggage.

Further, DnA coordinated with Moscow. For example, a report to the General Staff's office for intelligence revealed a secret agreement between DnA and Comintern, under which DnA accepted to undertake all orders from Moscow in exchange for political, financial, and military resources (Olstad, 1998, 39).

In 1922, the high court barrister and communist Ludvig Meyer was tasked to investigate the opportunities for revolutionary action. He concluded that "Norway is on the verge of breakdown, which can be exploited by a tax-strike and by pushing for demands that could rally the workers against the government. The Military and the [kings] guard was not as trustworthy as in 1921, and in the army perhaps, only as many as 3,000 men would go as far as to do their duty" (Olstad, 1998, 49). Meyer considered the Norwegian middle class "weak" and easy to contain through terror (Olstad, 1998, 49–50).

Despite Meyer perceiving a revolution as still likely, Comintern adherents in DnA had, by this time, started pushing for a more moderate line, following signals from the third international conference. Over time, this created a rift in DnA's revolutionary wing, which was exacerbated by Comintern demands that DnA submit to the twenty-one theses. Comintern, with its concept of parties organized as independent cells designed to operate in civil war–like environments, wanted DnA and AFL's dual membership revoked. Tranmæl and others wanted to use the dual membership of union and party to build a revolutionary movement "from below." Incidentally, Tranmæl's powerbase was split between the unions and the party. Together with Olaf Lian, he set about pushing the party to leave Comintern; DnA voted to leave in November 1923. The pro-Comintern fraction left the party congress immediately thereafter, establishing the Norwegian Communist Party (Norges Kommunistiske Parti [NKP]) the next day, with thirteen MPs defecting. In 1924, only six NKP MPs were reelected, reflecting the more general power shift back towards the reformists.

4.2 Elite Perception of the Likelihood of Revolution and Repressive Responses

We will now use various historical sources and statements made by different elites (often in private confidence) that clearly suggest the elites came to believe a revolutionary attempt by the radicals within the labor movement was a nonnegligible possibility. We then document the various repressive tactics aimed at reducing this threat.

The developments described in the previous sections were not lost on Norwegian economic and political elites. The revolution of 1917 and the following power change in DnA fundamentally altered perceptions of the labor movement and the security situation within the military and the business community, and among liberal and conservative political elites.

Figure 1 provides one barometer of how perceptions of the threat situation changed during this period. It reports annual frequencies of the terms "revolution," "Bolshevism," "general-strike" and "strikes" in articles in four major newspapers (*Aftenposten, Dagbladet, Morgenbladet,* and *Bergens Tidende*) read by various liberal and conservative elites. The overall pattern is increasing trends in the threat-perception terms from 1916/17 to 1919/20, and thereafter a notable decrease. This, more or less, tracks our interpretation of the perceptions of revolutionary threats from historians and archival and other source material.

Agøy (1994, 32–34) documents that, prior to 1917, the military establishment and political elites shared the opinion that one should avoid military engagement in internal affairs. By 1918, this had changed, along with increased perceptions of labor as a revolutionary threat. Within the general staff, major steps were taken to set-up "risk-free" military divisions – that is, excluding members from the lower classes (Agøy, 1994; Pettersen, 2010) – which could be mobilized during general strikes or strikes targeting strategic infrastructure. The secret police also decided to continue postage and telegram surveillance of

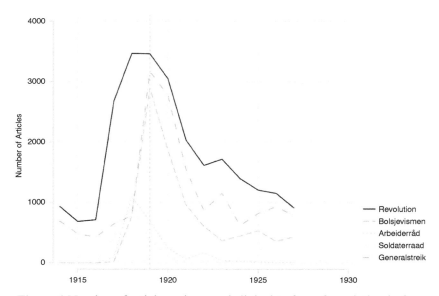

Figure 1 Number of articles using words linked to fear of revolution in four newspapers (*Aftenposten, Dagbladet, Morgenbladet,* and *Bergens Tidende*)

radical elements, despite it becoming illegal after 1918. Especially the circle around Martin Tranmæl was put under surveillance, and Tranmæl was later charged for working against the state. Military divisions and battleships would occasionally be mobilized as preemptive measures to avoid strikes from escalating. For example, the battleship *Harald Hårfagre* was sent to Trondheimsfjorden during strikes in 1918. The commander was told that "one must be prepared to face disturbances if the decision goes against the wishes of the workers" (Pettersen, 2010, 52). Similar preparations were in place during the railway strike of 1920.

The political elite was even more concerned than the military. Danielsen, the seminal historian on the Conservative Party, argued that the labor movement was viewed as the greatest regime threat since the Thrane movement more than seventy years earlier (Danielsen, 1984, 14–15). In early 1918, leading cabinet members feared an outright "coup" (Agøy, 1994, 94). The Liberal PM Gunnar Knudsen established a secret security commission, mandated to "secure peace and order if civilian government was brought down" and work to establish guidelines for cooperation between the different defense arms against the syndicalists (Pettersen, 2010, 43). The commission would operate in secret and as long as the threat persisted.

Knudsen was contacted by the employers' association, NAF, in mid-April 1918, which feared revolution following worker council meetings over the eight-hour-day issue. Knudsen's response was comforting to NAF: The military was prepared to intervene if necessary (Bjørnson, 1990, 549). Knudsen addressed the situation publicly in parliament on March 3: "It is tragic to have to say this, and even more tragic if one ends up having to do it; but the government is prepared [and if necessary,] ... strike fast." This, Knutsen continued, was better "than to show weakness and forbearance when facing possible breach of order, for then it might become so much worse later on."[14]

The security commission was summoned to reconvene on November 12, 1918, following revolutionary events in Germany, which convinced both the political establishment and especially the military that a revolutionary attempt was imminent in Norway (Agøy, 1997, 75). The military secret services and police were tasked to increase their surveillance and further develop plans for successful defense. Security talks (and later preparations) would especially focus on the role of strikers, who were assumed to aim at restricting the government's ability to control the country. Weapons stored in all army deposits around the country were to be made useless, and selected army units, excluding potential lower-class sympathizers, were prepared in secret (Agøy, 1997, 139).

---

[14] Stortingstidene 1918, March 3, p.399 (Gunnar Knudsen).

The size of these units is uncertain, but Agøy (1997, 118–119) estimated their strength at around 8,500 troops, supported by an additional 4,500, which was sizeable for Norwegian standards. Their equipment included machine guns (to ensure crowd control) and field artillery. Justice Minister Otto Blehrs summarized the response as follows:

> These present conditions must be given the highest priority of our police, and we must be prepared for attacks upon the government. A detailed plan for such an eventuality must be made and a written statement of such plans given to an amtsmann that could take over leadership of government and police if our current leaders were to be taken out. (Johansen, 1967, 9–10)

The government believed a revolutionary attempt was both possible and could result in the government being ousted.

After DnA's entry into Comintern, and with a national rail strike looming in 1920, fears of a revolution seemingly increased further among Norwegian political elites. The new Conservative PM Halvorsen discussed prospects of a revolution in a speech to fellow Conservative Party MPs:

> One is expecting the hardest of civil wars. . . . Our present enemy, even with their minority position, would still be able to win in the moment [and] we cannot know whether they intend to capture the positions of government. Edvard [Hagerup Bull] therefore said we must secure a government for the nation. He proposed that Ivar Lykke and Gunnar Knudsen should stand by with their people if anything were to set the current government out of play. If they and their people were to meet the same fate, the director general of the finance department should stand ready.
>
> (Danielsen, 1984, 18; translated by authors).

This speech strongly suggests that the revolutionary threat was perceived as credible; the Norwegian PM was, indeed, setting up lines of succession to a competitor party and the bureaucracy, because he believed the very existence of the regime was threatened.

Notably, the different elites coordinated their responses. The leading employer organization, NAF, coordinated with the government, which, in turn, coordinated with the security services (military and police arms). Our source material shows that all these elite groups considered revolution as a possibility throughout the period from 1918 to 1923, although revolution was considered more imminent in some years than others. For example, NAF seems to have been more concerned in 1918–19, and the government in 1918 and 1920 (Agøy, 1997).

The government also tried to respond to the increased threat by legislative means. A law on maintenance of "Public order during war and under the danger of war"[15] was put before parliament on March 9, 1918. It granted powers to the executive to act as if in wartime, when war was a possibility, and to define specific areas as zones of conflict, in which civil authorities could summon the military to maintain law and order. Additional surveillance measures were also proposed.

Among the Conservative and Liberal party members of the relevant parliamentary committee, none had any major objections to this initiative. In contrast, the representative of DnA (Aslaksrud) viewed the law as a severe intervention into citizens' civil rights and suggested it be withdrawn. Together with Johan Castberg (Social-Liberal MP) he argued that it broke with the constitution.[16] The proposal was eventually shelved after a heated exchange between Castberg and Liberal justice Minister Blehr.[17]

4.3 Eight-Hour Workday

We have detailed how several repressive measures were organized against the worker movement. Still our focus is on co-optive and integrative measures. These "silk glove responses" included several (proposed or implemented) reforms, such as proportional representation, subsidies for housing, firm councils, profit sharing, arbitration regulation, socialization of industries, generous unemployment subsidies, sickness benefits, and old-age pensions. In this section, we focus on how economic and political elites responded to the perceived labor threat by slowly accepting and ultimately promoting the implementation of the eight-hour workday.

Work hours were unregulated for adults in early-twentieth-century Norway. Several attempts to introduce legislation on the eight-hour day had been made in parliament since the Worker Commission of 1885. All failed. While many industrial countries had regulated hours for women, in Norway such proposals also met stark opposition, falling on roll-call votes in parliament after stiff and vocal employer protests. The only regulation applied to children.

In 1914, the "great reformer" of the Social-Liberal Party, Johan Castberg, made his second attempt (the first one in 1909 failed) to regulate working hours for adults.[18] At his behest, a proposition was put before the Storting, proposing a nine-hour workday with compensation for overtime, only to be postponed. In 1915, another attempt was made, but facing stiff employer resistance and heated exchanges in parliament; the resulting extensive changes to the act meant that

---

[15] Ot. prp. nr. 16. 1918; Indst. O. XIV 1918, p.1.   [16] Indst. O. XIV 1918, pp.3–4.

[17] Stortingstidene 1918, January 11.

[18] Proposals to set hours to forty-eight, fifty-six, fifty-eight and even seventy-two for men all fell in the Lagting and the Odelsting. (Stortingstidende 1909 efterm., July 6, pp.604–605, 620; Stortingstidede 1909, July 20, p.287).

the law ended up a major disappointment for its original architect. Gone was overtime compensation, daily hours were set to ten, and implementation to 1920, with major industries excluded. These changes prompted Castberg to note that one might as well drop the legislation.[19]

Another reality could have materialized. During the treatment of the paragraph on working time, DnA representative Ludvig Enge proposed that hours be set to eight. The proposal was downvoted seventy to twenty.[20] Only Socialists and Social-Liberals voted in favor. The nine-hour proposal from the committee was subsequently defeated with fifty-eight to thirty-two votes. Finally, the Liberal proposal of ten hours (a fifty-four-hour week), passed with seventy-four against sixteen votes.

Regarding the economic elites, the employer association NAF was, at the time, fully against *any* regulation of work hours in factories or the economy more generally. Any reductions in hours would be ruinous, destroying especially the capital-intensive industries.[21] The NAF even argued that the original act of 1909 was too encompassing and had to be reversed, and this law did not regulate hours at all. In fact, we have not identified a single employer speaking out in favor of regulating hours in conjunction with any of the proposed or undertaken reforms between 1900 and 1915.

The NAF was hesitant even in spring 1918, when commenting on a government proposal for a temporary eight-hour day. This was argued to "cause so many so many difficulties, that industrial stagnation or decline must be expected."[22] Yet, there had been movement within NAF, as, by 1918, it would not necessarily work against the implementation of such an act and NAF's position continued to change with perceptions of the revolutionary threat throughout 1918. Following revolutionary events in Finland and Germany, and the shift within the unions towards syndicalism, NAF eventually came to accept working-hour regulations both by legislation and in collective bargaining agreements. Especially NAF's CEO, Lars Rasmussen, argued for the necessity of meeting the workers' new ideological orientation by other means than force (Knutsen, 1994, 29–31). In his new-year's speech of 1919 to the board, Rasmussen outlined the dangers facing the organization, and the possible solution – accepting the eight-hour workday:

> Previously, our organization would respond to such demands with all the
> means at our disposal. But in this case, I believe, we must take into account,
> that behind these demands stand, so to speak, all the unrest that exists around

---

[19] Stortingstidene 1915 efterm., August 20, p.2368 (Castberg).
[20] Stortingstidene 1915 efterm., August 13, p.2172 (votering).
[21] Stortinget 1915, dokument 49, pp.25–33, 45–47, 115–123.
[22] Stortinget 1918, Indst O. XXIV 1918, p.1.

the earth at present, and it infects also our situation . . . For if we constrain this notion [that it's the workers' turn to win] too much, then the pressure might become too great. Then events will unfold without negotiations, and the result will be that the workers say: let us now seize the day, let us take power. Then we would be stuck in a societal upheaval, a situation that we would, by all means, seek to avert; we must be aware of the spirit of our times, we have to read its signs and learn its demands. We must therefore renege on some of our old principles. . ... We must make sure that we can save that which can be saved.[23]

Rasmussen seemingly reveals his inherent preference against the eight-hour day, noting that "before we would have resisted." Rasmussen's quote also suggests the reason for NAF still supporting the eight-hour day: it would integrate labor into the existing economic system, thereby mitigating risks of revolution. Previous hesitant voices and even outright antagonists such as Hydro factory owner Campbell-Andersen backed Rasmussen: "I agree that we must look at the signs of our time and therefore there is no use in resisting the eight-hour workday anymore."[24] Notably, all statements that we refer to by NAF members here originate from board notes, which were kept secret and meant to be destroyed later on (Knutsen, 1994). These quotes are therefore unlikely to represent strategic overtures to unions or empty rhetoric.

By 1919, various elites had thus shifted 180 degrees on the question of work-hour regulation. Both the Liberals and Conservatives had downvoted eight- and nine-hour workday proposals in 1915. Another attempt at introducing the eight-hour day in Parliament was made in 1918 but failed in producing a true eight-hour act. In 1915, 22 percent of MPs voted for an eight-hour law and 33 percent in 1918. In 1919, all parties would embrace the eight-hour day.

Gunnar Knudsen (PM, Liberal) decided at the end of 1918 that it was necessary to pass a true eight-hour bill to appease the socialists (Danielsen, 1984). On November 30, after the German revolution, Knudsen made it clear to NAF's leader that the eight-hour day was coming, and would be made into law "without any reservations" (Knutsen, 1994, 20). The social minister Berg (Liberals) opened the new parliament in 1919 by stating: "The times demand social reforms . . . we have great demands for social reforms, and the greatest task in my opinion, is that labor now takes precedence in our country.. . . Capital should be a servant and helper for labor, but not its master. It is this which is the demand of our time."[25]

When, on June 14 and July 2, 1919, a true eight-hour act was put forward to the two chambers of the Storting, it passed both in the lower (Odelsting) and

---

[23] NAF Sentralstyre January 12, 1919, p.4, Fure (1983, p. 506). Translated by authors.

[24] NAF Sentralstyre March 31, 1919, p.28 (Campbell-Andersen), quoted in Knudsen (1994 p. 49).

[25] Stortingstidene 1919 efterm., March 26, p.646 (Statsråd Berg).

higher chamber (Lagting) by *acclamation*. The change did not only reflect that new MPs (possibly with different preferences) had entered the Storting after the 1918 election. We matched names and voting records and checked how many of the MPs who opposed the 1918 proposal were reelected and accepted the 1919 proposal. In total, thirty-one MPs who had voted against the eight-hour workday were reelected, representing both the Liberal and Conservative parties. This is a stunning turnaround in a short period of time. What may have caused it?

The departmentally organized committee tasked to amend the factory act of 1915 highlighted the international situation as the key reason for reform:

> The powerful democratic wave that swept across Europe during the last years of the world war has created an ever-stronger demand for sweeping social reforms. And the 8-hour day is in all countries the one case that has been demanded resolved. Immediately after the first Russian revolution in 1917, an agreement was reached in Petrogad between the city's employers' association and the Workers' and Soldiers' Council, which, pending a general regulation of working hours, stipulated a factory working time of 8 hours and 8 hours on Saturday.[26]

The committee further highlighted the likelihood of labor conflicts if the eight-hour day was denied, and all participants (including NAF and other employer representatives) argued international developments made the eight-hour day inevitable.

The justifications put forward by parliamentarians themselves suggest that ensuring regime legitimacy among the working classes and social stability were important, both to Liberal and Conservative MPs. The Liberal government – here represented by social minister Berg – highlighted the high societal costs associated with trade unions struggle to achieve lower working hours through collective bargaining and that several collective agreements would expire in 1919, noting that "if the demand can be meet with legislation, much will have been won."[27] He went on to argue that

> It is imperative, for the sake of our society, that what can be done is done, to ensure that the workers can feel satisfied in their work, . . . it is, with the future in mind, of outmost importance for the satisfaction of the whole of society.. . . . With the eight-hour day implemented by law, our country's workers will find new faith in the notion that through a development of society as it now is, we can reach a societal-order where also they may find their place.[28]

The Conservatives in opposition were equally supportive. MP Klingenberg stated that, "we will now approve with law a demand that workers in the whole

---

[26] Departement for sociale saker, 1919, p.7.   [27] Ot. prp. nr. 21. 1919, p.8.
[28] Ot. prp. nr. 21. 1919, pp.8–9.

world, for a lifetime, have declared to be one of the most important to … achieve the social conditions under which they want to live and have a right to live under."[29]

The extent to which both Liberals and Conservatives supported the eight-hour day is remarkable considering the staunch opposition just four years prior. This sudden change of heart was noticed by the socialists. Nygaardsvold (DnA) would lament that, suddenly, all parties across the ideological spectrum had come to embrace what they had so vehemently fought against just four years ago:

> The road to legislative reform has been hard to travel. Each time the demand of the workers for an eight-hour normal working day was brought forward to the Storting, the demand was voted down, or the reform was so distorted that it would have no meaningful impact for the workers.… Workers therefore had to take on the issue themselves.… I want to add, that there is no single issue that has, to such an extent, made workers lose their faith in the parliamentary line, that parliamentary action work.… As long as workers did not put any major force behind their demand, the Storting voted down all proposals to reduce working-hours to 8 hours.[30]

Was the eight-hour day reform costly to the elites, or was it a cheap concession to make? We believe it was costly. The regulations forbid reducing daily wages, meaning the reform represented a major hourly wage increase for most workers. While we haven't quantified the impact, the contemporary reform in Sweden resulted in the greatest wage increase for Swedish industrial workers in modern history, with 1922 wages being 50 percent higher than before the reform (Bengtsson & Molinder, 2017). Since only 19.2 percent of *unionized* Norwegian workers worked forty-eight hours per week, with 67.4 percent working fifty-four hours or more in November 1918, most workers (and especially nonunionized), experienced a major reduction in hours and increased wages (AFL 1918, 204–205).

Granted, fear of a revolution was likely *not the only contributing factor* to the eight-hour act of 1919. It had become easier for proponents to promote a working-hour reform after the ILO and Versailles signatories had committed to the eight-hour day. Maintaining similar rules as the international manufacturing competition was therefore less of a relevant counterargument than before (Rasmussen, 2021). In addition, changes "on the ground" had occurred. The collective bargaining results of 1919 were quite generous; NAF accepted the eight-hour day, there were extensive wage increases, and paid leave was extended from four to six days in most agreements (AFL Beretning, 1919/20).

---

[29] Stortingstidene 1919, June 19, p.141.   [30] Stortingstidene 1919 efterm., July 2, p.64.

In the spring of 1919, NAF's Board decided that one *had to* avoid ending up in a major conflict;[31] concessions were required. NAF CEO Rasmussen argued that these concessions were a form of "insurance" necessary to ensure that no social upheavals took place, which could lead to things, of which we had no overview.[32] NAF would later summarize the results of the bargaining as having taken place under "the sign of the revolution."[33]

By 1920, the "good days" were over for the unions; Rasmussen had become convinced (in contrast with the government) that "the revolutionary waves that we feared last year would envelope us, have, in this year, leveled out somewhat."[34] NAF therefore demanded wage reductions in all collective agreements up for renegotiation in 1920.

The NAF proposals about wage reductions were perceived as nothing but a provocation by the unions. Negotiations stalled. Fearing the increased strife would escalate and spread, the government's answer was to use the Arbitration Act of 1915 (Fure, 1983, 578; Knutsen, 1994, 35). In so doing, the government pushed the fate of the negotiations into the hands of the worker-friendly chief justice of the Supreme Court, Karenus Kristofer Thinn. The Thinnian arbitration decisions – as they would be remembered – were excruciating for the employers. The previous six days of paid leave became fourteen, and further wage increases came across the board. Fure (1983, 578) argues that this was the last true "appeasement policy" pursued by the political establishment during this period.

The 1922 bargaining rounds would be nothing like that of 1921. Gone was Thinn, and as the unions launched "a great showdown" with the employers, hopeful to force fundamental reforms, they found that they had overestimated their strength. Pervasive use of strikebreakers and the absence of a general mobilization in the population contributed to a decisive defeat (Bjørgum, 1985, 92). Close to all agreements that were up for renegotiation ended with major wage decreases and vacation days were reduced to eight (AFL Beretning, 1922, 23). Clearly, the unions' bargaining power was on the decline in 1922, and this realization would become paramount for elites in deciding on further responses to worker demands.

4.4 Socialization of Means of Production, Worker Participation in Management, and Profit Sharing

This section considers elite support for socialization of property and the various attempts to legislate employee representation in management or boards through

---

[31] NAF Sentralstyre, April 24, 1919, p.7 (Schuman), quoted in Knudsen (1994, p. 29).

[32] NAF Sentralstyre, January 20. p. 4–5 (Rasmussen), quoted in (Fure 1983, p. 507 and Knudsen 1994, p. 30).

[33] Arbeidsgiveren, 1. 1920, 3. Oslo.

[34] NAF Sentralstyre, January 20, 1920, p.7 (Rasmussen) quoted in Knudsen (1994, p. 35).

company councils. We highlight how proposals passed unanimously in parliament during periods of revolutionary fear, but later proposals were dead on arrival after the revolutionary period had passed.

No proposal would be so radical, and potentially so transformative for the Norwegian economy, as those pertaining to socialization of means of production and property. The most radical proposals were that firms would become state owned and managed through a system of councils at the firm and sector levels. While these proposals would amount to nothing but government reports, they constituted a different vision for Norwegian society and economy than the existing capitalist system. The mere fact that they were entertained by elites, speaks volumes about the perceived threat after the Bolshevik Revolution. Once the revolutionary threat dissipated, elites quickly eliminated any chance of a legislative proposal on socialization.

The socialization proposals became embroiled in questions of worker participation in management. Together, these proposals challenged the very foundation of the economic elite's interests and power, namely their property and right to manage that property. A third option, profit-sharing, was also discussed, but then by the elites as a counterresponse to the more radical proposals.

Prior to 1918, the involvement of workers in firm management or socialization of property were anathema among Norwegian political and economic elites.[35] With the Bolshevik Revolution of November 1917 and the adoption of a radical line within DnA in 1918, the debate changed drastically. The Norwegian worker movement, spearheaded by Tranmæl, advocated the formation of company councils ("Bedriftsråd") within an overarching frame of branch and national councils. These were conceptualized as decision-centers: management of firms and whole industries were to be shifted into the councils as a first step to socialization (Petersen, 1950, 337–338). This broke with NAF's "fundamental principles" against which the employers were ready to mobilize "the whole strength of the federation" (Petersen, 1950, 337–338).

While the business elites did not intend to play ball, the political elites took the initiative to pursue the question. Facing the changing situation of 1918, the Liberal government proposed to deal with the increasing conflict over profits in the traded sector by distributing employee dividends. This strategy would deflect the issue from socialization to a question of profit sharing, turning workers into capitalists. This new position was launched in the Opening of Parliament speech ("Trontalen") in 1918, and was even supported by the leader of the Conservative group in parliament:

---

[35] St. prp. nr. 134, p.1. 1918.

What is unfortunate is ... that the traded interests have taken out exorbitant dividends. Furthermore, it is unappealing that the traded interests also under these favorable conditions have held their employees' wages down at such a level ... it is completely unjustified.... The state cannot stand indifferent in the face of these hardships. For these reasons, I find it regrettable that no employer has even in such a restricted extent experimented with having their employees revising dividends or share in the companies themselves.... I now view with satisfaction that the government party now wants to address this issue.[36]

It was also supported by Peterson (Conservative, factory owner), who linked dividends explicitly to the possibility of lessening current worker troubles:

I would say that if there exist antidotes that are congruent with our view of capitalist society, which can also bring in an additional element of greater social peace, greater trust, and greater harmony interests between capital and labor, between the factory and its workers. ... Many have argued that we have the solution in the dividend system.... The government should put down a commission to evaluate this question.[37]

Subsequently, the government set down a commission to evaluate "the question of employer dividends and share of management." The aim was social preservation; "to create a closer community of interest between industrial firms and their workers by making these partake in the company's capital and dividends as well as their management."[38] It was later renamed the Worker Commission of 1918 (WC), and put forward legislative proposals on work councils (1919, 1920) and profit-sharing schemes (1922). In the end, the only real impact was the temporary act on work councils of 1920, which would have little to no consequence for Norwegian firms.

The Socialization Commission (SC) of 1919 was even more radical. Its task was to evaluate the question of socialization, both in industry and the mining sector (Danielsen, 1984, 19). Several WC members also participated in the SC. In addition, a Land Commission of 1919 was set-up to discuss the issue of inequality in arable land. Its primary task was to assess the possibility of procuring land for tenant farmers. Yet, little came out of its efforts.

In early 1919, the WC was to develop a legislative proposal on employee participation in management. It quickly split into a majority consisting of worker representatives and academics, and a minority consisting of business leaders. The majority proposed the establishment of a system of firm, district,

---

[36] Stortingstidene 1918 efterm., March 16 – trontaledebatten, p.534 (Bull).
[37] Stortingstidene 1918 efterm., March 16 – trontaledebatten, pp.596–597 (Peterson).
[38] St. prp. Nr. 134, p.1. 1918

and national work councils. Work councils would have executive power over work schedules, procurement of technology, and hiring of supervisors.[39] The minority preferred a system of firm-specific councils with advisory roles. The minority position was put forward to parliament by the Halvorsen (Conservative) government in 1920 – with certain small modifications – and enacted without dissent.

In 1922, the WC outlined its proposed company council scheme and its proposal on profit sharing. The group split again, with the commission writing two major opposing legislative proposals. The majority position proposed profit sharing in all firms (public and private), except in the primary industries. Dividends would be paid proportionally in wages and "capital wages," the latter being set by each firm. More radically, they proposed a fund, financed by taxes on profits exceeding 10 percent, for buying up defunct firms and establishing new ones. This proposal was dead on arrival (Petersen, 1950, 355).

Even with only the limited proposals winning support in parliament, the business elites were dismayed. The NAF considered the 1920 Work Council act "pure madness" as an economic policy, but as a defensive measure against syndicalist tendencies and revolutionary threats, it made sense.[40] Still, NAF and employers did not publicly convey their preferences. Instead, they stated that such a reform "would create greater job satisfaction and increase work perform-ance" (Danielsen, 1984, 32). NAF leaders were even more negative to the design of the 1922 profit-sharing scheme. In 1918, NAF had set down its own commission to evaluate the profit-sharing question (Petersen, 1950, 350). Its conclusion in 1921 stated that while voluntary forms could be implemented, "it is unimaginable that a compulsory arrangement can be implemented with satisfactory results" (Petersen, 1950, 352). Still, NAF saved its hardest criticism for the socialization proposals, "which only built on unsatisfactory knowledge of the most simple and elementary social and economic conditions, and one could only regret that the abovementioned fraction did not have the necessary insight on this area."[41]

The radicals within DnA, on the other hand, were concerned with the dangers of an elite-initiated reform on company councils. If the councils were to focus only on specific aspects of production and have advisory functions, their role as revolutionary institutions would be limited (DnA, 1920). They would instead facilitate "conciliation between the classes" (DnA, 1920, 76). Instead, DnA supported the WC majority's proposal, which would have given the workers

---

[39] Ot. prp. nr. 65. 1920.
[40] NAF Sentralstyre, August 23, 1920, p.20 (Rasmussen) quoted in Knutsen (1994, p. 51).
[41] Expert from the NAF run newsmagazine *Arbeidsgiveren*, November 24. Cited in Peterson (1950, 355).

greater influence over company decisions. Perhaps surprisingly, the unions advocated *against* profit sharing, considering that it would adversely affect worker solidarity within industries and reduce support for the centralized collective bargaining system (and thus wage improvements in low-profit firms).

As the fear of revolution subsided after the early 1920s, the political elite shifted again on the question of socialization. The Conservatives, which had all voted for the continuation of the SC up until 1922, would in 1923 abruptly change their perception on its necessity. The SC was defunded and its mandate reduced to give a theoretical elaboration of the question of socialization. Labor party representatives put forward counterproposals, pleading with the relevant head of committee (Lykke, Conservatives) "not to start class-warfare on an evaluation of a question such as this."[42]

Lykke's proposal won out against the combined vote of the various labor parties. Was Lykke acting in good faith and just restraining a committee that had gone overboard by more precisely stating its mandate? We find this unlikely. First, Lykke had showed no problem with WC and SC previously, and had even been a WC member before entering government in 1920. The committee had been granted the funding it asked for each year up to 1923, without complications. It is more likely that, after the revolutionary threat dissipated, Lykke and others now felt confident enough to push back against the prior "appeasement policies."

Such a change is also traceable in the party manifestos of the Conservative Party. Between 1909 and 1915, the manifestos exclude any mention of co-ownership or co-management. The manifesto of 1918 is unique, stating that the co-ownership issue must be "evaluated and solved" (Høire, 1918). These lines did not make it into the 1924 manifesto. The change in position is startling if viewed as a change in ideology. However, it fits very neatly with our perspective on strategic responses to revolutionary pressure.

The work of the commissions discussed in this section would, in the end, amount to little. The proposals came to parliament at a time in when the revolutionary threat was on the decline, both domestically and internationally. It is therefore unsurprising that the elites worked hard to ensure that nothing was to come from the quite radical proposals proposed by these commissions.

4.5 Old-Age Pensions

Another policy victory that would end up being ephemeral for workers, was the promise of an old-age pension program. Norway was among the last industrialized countries to implement government-regulated old-age pension. An old-age

---

[42] Stortingstidene 1923 efterm., March 23 – kommisjonsbudgsjettet, p.673 (Gjøstein).

pension program was proposed already in 1844, followed by similar proposals starting in 1854 and finally a more formal proposal originating in the Worker Commission of 1894. These proposals resulted in nothing. In 1907, the People's Insurance Committee was charged to evaluate the question. It handed in two proposals that would frame the pension debate for the near future: a tax-financed proposal favored by DnA and an insurance scheme favored by the Liberal Party. The proposals went nowhere, and no proposition was put to a vote in parliament.

Coinciding with the revolutionary situation in 1918, the Liberal government unveiled the first royal proposition on an age and disability pension scheme, based on the earnings-related scheme. The proposition was treated in parliament in 1919. The Conservatives were highly critical of the proposed scheme, as it implied an extensive bureaucracy. DnA wanted a more progressive system and pensions and benefits from day one. Thus, the Storting unanimously decided to evaluate a tax-proposal to go along with the Liberals' earnings-related alternative. This was the first time parliament had agreed on the principle of old-age pensions.

Before 1919, the conservatives had always preferred an earnings-related system, but now they sided with DnA in pushing for a tax-based system. As with the introduction of PR (described in the next section), this was an initiative from the party leadership (Pettersen, 1978, 13). The aim was to create a society-preserving institution, using the old-age pension as a basic security without the stigma of poor relief (Danielsen, 1984, 30). A tax-alternative was handed in by 1920, but the government fell before it could put forth a proposal. In October 1920, the new Liberal government put forward a proposition outlining a new version of the earnings-related scheme. In January 1921, Halvorsen (Conservative) put forward a revised tax-scheme proposal. The situation ended up in a vote that led to postponement. Treatment of the two proposals was attempted during summer 1923, but it was again postponed, until October, when it survived postponement proposals in the Odelsting and finally made its way to the Lagting.

When reaching the Lagting on November 30, 1923, discussion and disagreement was still prevalent. Liberal MP Høgseth decried the increasing burden of state and municipality budgets, accusing the proponents of the tax system of communism. Social Minister Klingenberg (Conservative) was harsh in his reply, exclaiming, "No, this has nothing to do with communism or socialism.... If it is anything, it is policy aimed at the preservation of society!"[43]

---

[43] Stortingstidende 1923 efterm., November 30, p.257.

The Social Democrat Magnussen also underlined the consequences of postponement:

> One talks so often in these times about the working class and its attitude to the parliamentary system of governance, its position on parliamentarianism. I think that one should consider the consequences of saying no to a reform such as this. One should not disappoint the working class, which has put its hope and trust to parliamentarianism and is waiting on what the Lagting decides. One should think not just once, but two and three times over.[44]

Yet, with the failure of the DnA proposal, the remaining question was simply whether the government would commit to a principle for how old-age pensions would be organized. Eventually, the tax-based option was chosen by the combined efforts of DnA, many Conservatives, and some Liberals.

The old-age pension's proposal would mark the end of a long line of social policy proposals initiated by conservative and liberal politicians to starve the revolutionary beast. At the time, trade union organization had declined to prewar levels, the failed great strike of 1922 showed the difficulties of workers pursuing the radical line, and DnA would leave Comintern in 1923. Internationally, the Red Army had already been defeated in Poland and the failed revolutionary uprising in Bulgaria in 1923 only reinforced the notion that the "World Revolution" was, indeed, dead.

Fittingly, the 1923 act on pensions was never even brought before the Storting for a vote on implementation. Old-age pensions had to wait another thirteen years. In 1936, Nygaardsvold (DnA) had become PM for a minority government. He dusted off the old proposal of 1923, reduced the level of benefits, and finally pushed it through parliament.

4.6 Institutional Change

While our focus in this Element is on how revolutionary threat perceptions lead to social and economic policy change, a similar logic applies to institutional change. We discuss suffrage extension and the introduction of proportional representation in light of our argument.

4.6.1 Suffrage Extension

Norway had already implemented universal male suffrage in 1898, with women receiving full voting rights in 1913. However, with the 1898 constitutional amendment, §52d stated that poor relief recipients were determined unqualified as voters. This group increased over time, especially with the extension of the vote to women.

---

[44] Stortingstidende 1923 efterm., November 30, p.264.

Some 4.2 percent of the population (almost twice as many women as men) had their voting rights suspended due to receiving poor relief aid in 1915. This rule was frowned upon by many reform-minded liberals and others.

In 1916, three constitutional amendments that, in varying degrees, made poor relief recipients eligible to vote reached parliament. A Liberal government proposal went the furthest, proposing to outright abolish the rule. DnA, afraid the government proposal would fail, proposed to circumscribe the rule's impact, making exceptions for poor relief recipients based on old age, disability, unemployment, and sickness.

The opposition position was summarized by the conservatives Norløff and Thallaug:

> We cannot join the majority position. The majority builds its considerations on the claim that the right to vote is a universal right to all that are free humans and members of our society, that have not been found guilty of criminal actions. The minority is not in agreement with this consideration.... It is wrong and questionable that persons that can provide for themselves, but have chosen not to, shall keep their right to vote. They have deserved to lose the right to vote.[45]

In parliament, the roll calls ended up with a narrow defeat for the Liberal proposal, with Liberal Party unity breaking down as farmer MPs voted together with a uniform conservative opposition. The more moderate DnA proposal gained the necessary two-thirds majority for passage.

In 1919, the Constitutional Commission would unanimously recommend outright removing §52D. The commission argued that, "It is in everyone's interest, and completely in line with the modern, humane view of society, that legislation does not no place an additional heavy burden on the already heavy burden that is borne by the poor."[46]

The proposal passed parliament without any opposing votes nor any noticeable debate,[47] which marked a change in position for the conservatives and liberal farmer MPs from just three years prior. However, we cannot provide any direct evidence supporting that revolutionary fear contributed to this change in preferences. Another possible explanation is that the modifications enacted in 1916 had made the paragraph unworkable, leading to various misunderstandings by local election officials.[48]

4.6.2 Electoral Rule Reform

The introduction of a proportional electoral system was a key demand of DnA, especially following the rise of the anti-parliamentarian radicals in the party.

---

[45] Indst. S. nr. 142, 1916, pp.1, 5.   [46] Indst. S. nr. 279, 1919, p.4.
[47] Stortingstidene 1919 efterm., July 17, pp.2523–2524.   [48] Ibid.

Table 1 Percentage of MPs voting in favor of removing runoffs and keeping SMD

Proposal	DnA	Liberal Party	Conservative Party	Overall
1913 vote	100	19	85	50
1917 vote	100	15	72	40

Both reformists and radicals perceived the single member district (SMD) runoff system of 1905 as highly unjust. Over time, this system led to an increasing gap between the percentages of votes and parliamentary seats for DnA. This discrepancy was especially driven by the runoff component of the system, as it allowed Liberals and Conservatives to coordinate on the candidate best placed to defeat DnA candidates in the second round. As shown by Fiva and Hix (2021), these parties only failed to coordinate in one instance, meaning that DnA typically ended up losing even where it had a plurality of votes.

The disproportionality of the SMD system didn't mean DnA reformists supported PR. They envisioned a road to a socialist society through achieving majority within the SMD system, as the increasing number of workers and trade unionist would secure socialist majorities against a fractured elite. But the runoff part of the system had to go. Between 1905 and 1918, the party leadership made two attempts to remove the runoff. Table 1 shows the percentage of MPs from the different parties voting in favor of removing the runoff. Following the defeat of the proposal (which required a super-majority for being changed), DnA party secretary Magnus Nilssen again proposed the exact same reform on December 2, 1917 (cosponsored with other reformists). The various proposals for changing to a PR system also put forward in this period had no DnA cosigners.

Radicals within DnA concluded that the existing parliamentary system was illegitimate, systematically repressing labor representation, and that reforming it was futile. For example, the radical editor Olausson argued that a revolution was necessary, as attempts to reform the system would only engender civil war:

> We see that the bourgeoisie has acquired weapons. Does one believe that they will give up their struggle? No, I do not think so. Then we will have a civil war.... We cannot achieve electoral majority with the current electoral system, and the bourgeoisie knows this. Therefore they will resist a just electoral system, if necessary, with arms. (DnA, 1918, 61–62)

Radicals instead wanted to pursue a strategy of soldier- and worker-council formation, and use said councils as governing institutions, replacing the parliamentary system.

With the radicals' takeover of the DnA leadership in 1918, the grievances related to the electoral system, and the threat they presented, didn't go unnoticed by elites. The leading conservative politician Fredrik Stang publicly stated that it was paramount that a new electoral system be introduced during 1919 to remedy the current injustices for the socialists. At the front page of the leading conservative newspaper *Aftenposten*, on December 15, 1918, he wrote: "It is dangerous to maintain this parliament, elected by a system judged unjust by the people.... The great danger, which is now rising, is the demand for the dictatorship of the few ... The choice is between electoral reform or revolution and civil war followed by a worker dictatorship." Danielsen (1984, 19) notes that the ensuing "electoral reform can stand as a key example ... of the conciliatory strategy," and specifies that Liberal and Conservative party leaders, in preparation to the vote on electoral reform, had decided that introducing PR would contribute to avoiding revolution.

Why did reformist social democrats end up supporting PR? It was the rise of the radicals and their takeover of the party that shifted reformists to support PR as a second-best solution. Needing to shore up support for the parliamentary strategy, reformists saw PR as the best solution to achieve quick correspondence between votes and seats, and to revitalize the parliamentary strategy in the face of the council strategy of the radicals.

The constitutional amendment on PR had been put forward to the Storting on December 12, 1917, and would be treated after the next election (1918). In early 1919, the treatment of the election commission's proposals was postponed to the end of the year. This led to a heated response, with the now radical-dominated DnA threatening to withdraw socialist MPs from parliament, or to carry out an "election-strike."

The parliamentary debate on November 28–29, 1919, provides further evidence that PR was introduced as a concession to ensure the integration of workers into the current system and mitigating revolutionary threats. The party-leaders had already bargained between themselves, deciding on implementing some form of PR, even if they were highly split on the specific electoral rules. The DnA representative in the Electoral Commission, Magnus Nilssen, drew the big picture:

> In 1918 we witnessed that strong forces would make themselves known within the worker movement.... We who have participated in the Electoral Commission were under the strong impression ... that time was of the essence in getting a grand proposal ready.... At meetings and in the press, people from all parties presented the injustice and risk of continuing an electoral system under which especially DnA was so unjustly treated ... I am in no doubt that if parliament were to enact a postponement, it would do itself a disservice.... I am highly confident that there will be raised a strong, public and justified

sentiment against parliament, if it does not take to its senses and vote on the current proposition. We all know how the situation has been in nearby countries, and we have seen the waves wash up on our shores, and if we are serious in governing our country by legislation and by the parliamentary ways, our duty demands that we, as quickly as possible, arrange the parliamentary institutions in such a way that the people can be satisfied with it.[49]

Liberal Party leader and Prime Minister, Gunnar Knudsen, would, albeit in more careful terms, draw similar connections between the nature of the electoral system and the order of society, in his reply to a DnA MP:

It was shown that the party he belonged to didn't receive even half of the representative that it should have received in proportion to its size of the electorate.... [A]ll parties recognized that circumstances have become such, that this could no longer go on and that it was necessary to establish a better electoral system, a more just electoral system ... instead of 41 representatives, that party received 18. It is nothing to be startled over, that such a result can create unwillingness and indignation and awaken thoughts, which do not go together with a well ordered society.[50]

Previously, Knudsen had constituted one of the major obstacles of PR. He resisted overtures for electoral reform between 1911 and 1915, and his change of heart coincided with the adoption of the revolutionary line by DnA. His first admissions to some form of electoral rule change came in August 1918, four months after the leadership change in DnA, when he referenced the radicalization of labor.

The following year he would push his party to accept some form of proportional representation, starting with a speech in Skien in which he noted the advance of bolshevism in Norway through DnA and the rising discontent with the unjust electoral system. He went as far as arguing that if the socialists demanded new elections under PR, this should be pursued to reduce social strife.[51] At the Liberal Party congress in June, he directly tied the radicalization of DnA to the need for electoral system reform: "The current [electoral] system is obviously unjust. Especially is this the case for the socialists, ... their votes only count in the election statistics. Under these conditions, discontent among the socialists has skyrocketed. As a result, the revolutionaries have taken control of the party."[52]

Following his recommendation, the party congress ended up voting that: "The Liberal party congress recommends that Stortorget enacts an electoral system that secures a more just distribution of representatives.... This should be

---

[49] Stortingstidene 1919, November 28, pp.2878–2883.
[50] Stortingstidene 1919, November 28, p.2930.
[51] Speech Skien, June 9. Referenced in *Dagbladet*, June 10, 1919, p.1.
[52] Referenced in *Romsdals Budstikke*, June 26, 1919, p.1.

achieved through a system of multimember districts under proportional representation."[53]

Leader of the Conservative Party, Halvorsen argued along similar lines: "We demand of all parties that they follow the parliamentary line. It is consequently decisive that we then open up for equal access to all parties to pursue their interests within parliament.... The times demand it." Several similar considerations are also found in the statements of individual Conservative and Liberal Party MPs.

While different electoral concerns and other motivations may also have mattered (see Gjerløw & Rasmussen, 2022 for a review of alternative explanations), the introduction of PR in Norway thus seems partly motivated by mitigating the revolutionary threat. The election of 1921 had a profound impact on DnA. Tranmæl himself admitted that interest in parliamentary means for the workers' class struggle got new wind in its sails following the electoral victory (Gjerløw & Rasmussen, 2022). We refer to Gjerløw and Rasmussen (2022) for a more detailed discussion of this relationship, and different types of evidence linking revolutionary threat perceptions to the electoral system reform.

4.5 Summary

The Bolshevik Revolution helped spur different repressive and appeasing policy changes in Norway between 1918 and 1923. Following our expectations, labor's international organizational linkages were an important factor behind Norwegian elites ascertaining a high level of revolutionary threat. In reports and discussions, membership in international organizations such as Comintern were used as indicators of revolutionary sentiment among workers and their organizations.

Various sources and pieces of evidence support the hypothesis that social policies were often born out of elite fears of worker revolution. The Bolshevik Revolution and subsequent DnA membership in Comintern fueled radical factions in the Norwegian labor movement, and thus the perception of labor as a potential revolutionary force. A combination of repressive and inclusionary tactics – especially pursuing social policy concessions that benefitted urban workers – was developed by elites to weaken radical groups and strengthen reformists in DnA.

Regarding the policy concessions, we have highlighted the eight-hour workday. This policy had been a key demand from workers for several decades but was only passed – and then unanimously – after the increase in revolutionary threat. Once implemented, the policy was not reversed after the revolutionary threat dissipated. The same was true for other policy and institutional changes,

---

[53] Minutes from the party congress referenced by *Nationen*, June 25, 1919, pp.2–3.

such as the introduction of PR. In contrast, policy concessions that were only discussed but never implemented, such as those pertaining to the socialization of means of production, were soon shelved once the elites perceived that the revolutionary threat dissipated.

5 Measuring Social Policies and Revolutionary Threat across Countries

Despite the strong fit between the Norwegian case and many of our theoretical expectations, there is no guarantee against Norway being an outlier. If we want to draw general conclusions, we must test implications from our theory on a wider set of cases. While our more cursory reading of the histories of other countries assuages concerns that Norway is "unique" (see online Appendix A4[54] for an overview of developments in selected European countries), it is infeasible to make similar in-depth analyses of several countries. Instead, we use an alternative strategy and "go broad," testing additional implications from our argument on revolutionary threat perceptions and policy concessions on global, cross-country data. To this end, we have coded new country-level measures on labor regulation and social policies, which we use alongside existing ones. In this section, we describe these data. But first, we discuss our main independent variable:

5.1 Measuring Revolutionary Threat

We have coded the formation of soldier- and worker councils in different countries as proxies of revolutionary threat (perceptions). Yet, our main measure draws on the observation that Trotsky, in January 1919, invited several revolutionary groups to Moscow to set up Comintern (Carr, 1979). Invitations did not include all labor organizations, and were not randomly distributed, but only sent to truly radical worker groups (to avoid "ideological contamination").

This feature allows us to distinguish contexts where labor had adopted a radical ideology from others context. Not only should we consider Trotsky's invitations a valid "expert opinion" on which countries faced revolutionary pressures in 1918–19, they also provided clear signals to elites that domestic labor groups were revolutionary threats. Being invited to the Comintern presented a clear and observable signal – anecdotally, the Comintern membership of DnA dominated several front pages of conservative Norwegian newspapers – about radical ideology and revolutionary intent. Further, we discussed in Section 3 how participating in the Comintern may even have had independent effects on the actual motivation as well as capacity to organize revolution among partaking

---

[54] Appendices available online at www.cambridge.org/

movements. Comintern invitations and participation should therefore capture various features that correlate with high perceived levels of revolutionary threat by the elites.

Regarding our specific measures, these are, first, an indicator for whether a union or party from the country was *invited* to the first Comintern meeting, and, second, an indicator for whether a party or union from the country *attended* this meeting with voting rights. We use the invitation measure as our main measure since it does not hinge on the active choice of domestic unions or parties to partake in the meeting and is therefore "more exogenous." The participation measure is used for robustness tests. Both measures take (invitations and attendance at) the first Comintern meeting as point of departure. For more details, we refer to Appendix A1, and we refer to Appendix A3 for descriptive statistics for this and all other variables entering the main analyses in the next chapter.

The main reason for using such a simple dichotomous specification on at least one union/party being invited or not as a main measure, is to mitigate the difficulty of ascertaining how much extra weight to put on additional representatives being invited to Comintern, and how to normalize according to, for example, population size. The two consultative delegates from China at the first Comintern meeting exceeded the lone Bulgarian delegate, but it is not obvious that this indicates "greater representation" of China, given the large population difference. Thus, we mainly use the simple dummy variable set-up, but our main results are robust to using continuous measures on number of attendees (Appendix A8).

Concerning measurement validity, we readily acknowledge that the Comintern-based measures are not direct measures of elite perceptions of revolutionary threat, and also that they provide limited time-series variation for each country. (But we use different strategies to account for this limited variation and control for other potentially relevant factors that also tended to change during the same period). Nonetheless, reliable, alternative measures for revolutionary threat are, unfortunately, hard to come by. To our knowledge, no encompassing dataset on political strikes or communist party membership exists for the relevant time interval.[55] If our Comintern measures are very "noisy," the corresponding regression coefficients will most likely be attenuated, making it harder to find support for our theoretical expectations. (In bivariate regressions, unsystematic measurement errors always lead to attenuation bias, but exceptions might occur in multivariate analysis).

---

[55] The often-used Banks data on general strikes draws on one source (*New York Times*) and does not capture lockouts or strikes per se, and general strikes only sparingly. To illustrate, in 1919, Norway experienced its greatest strikes and lockout waves (to that point), but is assigned zero strikes. Even more concerning, the massive general strikes in 1920 and 1923 are not captured.

Still, we want to assess the robustness of the relationships across different (albeit imperfect) measures. One alternative indicator of Bolshevik-inspired political mobilization is the presence of worker- and soldier councils; the Zimmerwald declaration following the Russian Revolution explicitly encouraged the formation of such councils to spread the revolution (Nordvik, 1974). We collected new data also on worker- and soldier councils, creating a dummy variable that registers if a country experienced the formation of at least one council during 1918–19. The data sources, even for countries with extensive council formation, do not allow us to register when these councils became defunct, but they tended to ebb out by the early 1920s (Nordvik, 1974). We use this measure in robustness tests. Convergent validity tests with the worker- and soldier council measure suggest that our main Comintern measure is a valid indicator of revolutionary threat. Only four countries with Comintern invitations did *not* have council movements – Brazil, Turkey, Portugal, and Spain – whereof the two former had pervasive riots, general strikes, and protests organized by syndicalist unions between 1917 and 1920.

5.2 Dependent Variables

Our argument highlights that elites are likely to target policy benefits that mitigate grievances among the urban working classes. For our dependent variable, we require measures that capture policies benefitting this group.

First, we coded a measure for "normal weekly working hours" for factory (industrial) workers, defined as the number of hours an employee can work before overtime restrictions come into play. This is our main dependent variable. Absent regulation, we code seventy-two hours per week (12 hours*6 days); results are robust to alternative assumptions. For the sources used and details on this measure (e.g. on handling sectoral differences within manufacturing), we refer to Appendix A2.

Our alternative measures pertain to the eligibility for coverage *or* generosity of social transfer programs that were key to mitigating work-life risks. Our argument pertains to the threat stemming from urban industrial workers, and we thus focus on coverage for this group. Hence, our second measure captures the extent to which industrial workers are protected against central work-life risks; old-age, sickness, maternity, accidents, unemployment, and child-rearing. Eligibility for coverage for a specific risk can be issued through various programs. Our measure considers the different provisions that are possible, and that multiple programs tend to increase coverage (within the relevant group). Yet, given the differences between programs in the likelihood of providing efficient coverage and insurance for low-income groups, our measure only considers four types of redistributive programs, namely social insurance, voluntary state-subsidized insurance, noncontributory with means-testing, noncontributory without means-testing. We thus exclude nonredistributive programs such as mandatory private accounts, employer liability, and lump-sum provident schemes. The theoretical range of this measure is 0 (industrial workers covered in no program) to 24 (industrial workers covered for all six risks in all four relevant types of redistributive programs; 6*4=24). Yet, the empirical range is far more limited in our main analysis, typically extending from 0–5.[56]

Social transfer programs may formally cover social groups without channeling substantial resources to recipients. Thus, our final dependent variables capture the generosity of core welfare programs, measuring duration of benefits for sickness and unemployment, respectively. Unfortunately, these measures are only coded for 1925 and we present these results in Appendix A10. Briefly, these tests paint the same picture as tests on the other dependent variables; countries that faced high revolutionary threats obtained more generous programs than other countries.

5.3 Benchmark Specification

We highlight at the outset that our results are robust to using cross-section or panel data, different estimation techniques, sets of controls, error correction methods, etc. For our benchmark, we opt for a simple OLS specification. When run on panel data, we cluster errors by country to account for panel-level serial correlation. We prefer a dual fixed effects specification, including dummies for both countries and years, which eliminates several hard-to-measure confounders that may simultaneously affect both revolutionary risk and social policy provision and design. For example, some countries, for historical or geographical reasons, could have industrial production concentrated in certain sectors that both facilitate the coordination of strong unions and provide an impetus for broad social policy coverage. In the benchmark, we include logged GDP per capita (p.c.) to account for level of development; GDP p.c. should also correlate with productivity and extent of industrialization. The GDP p.c. estimates are from Fariss et al. (2017). These imputed data with extensive time series come from a dynamic latent trait model on various data sources, and mitigate measurement errors of various kinds. We also control for log population (also from Fariss et al., 2017).

In alternative specifications, we include country-specific trends or a lagged dependent variable (LDV). We also use an instrumental variable design, using

---

[56] We also test measures for whether industrial workers are covered in redistributive programs for each risk, separately (Appendix A7).

signatories on the proclamation of the Zimmerwald group to instrument for Comintern invitations. We detail these (and other) alternative specifications when they are used in the following section.

6 Statistical Analysis

6.1 Main Cross-Country Analysis on Work Time Regulation

We probe the generalizability of our argument, first, by testing implications on what patterns of work-time regulation we should observe in cross-country data. We carry out several (quite demanding) tests on both cross-section data and panel data, controlling for several, plausible alternative explanations. Some of the tests resemble a difference-in-differences logic, as we draw on information from both treated countries (invitations to Comintern in 1919) and nontreated ones, pre- and post-1919.

To sum up the results, countries facing an increased revolutionary threat, following Comintern invitations (or erection of soldier- and worker councils), on average, limited working time by substantially more hours in the succeeding years. We also find that the estimated effects of this "revolutionary shock" lingered on; states that experienced greater revolutionary threat in 1919 had lower working hours even at the end of the Cold War. We will now go into more detail on the different tests and results:

For starters, the cross-section regressions in Table 2 show a strong and robust relationship between revolutionary threat perception, proxied by Comintern invitations, and working hours. Model 1, a sparse model without any controls, shows that "Comintern countries" had about 10.8 fewer working hours per week than other countries in 1919 (results are stable to forward-lagging the dependent variable). In Model 2 we control for log GDP p.c. and log population. The predicted difference in hours then increases to 11.4. This result is visualized in a partial-regression leverage plot (Figure 2), displaying the relationship between Comintern invitations and working hours after taking out the variation that both factors have in common with the controls.

In extension, we use the technique developed by Xu et al. (2019), and check how many observations must be miscoded for this result to be invalidated. More than half of our countries (45/87) would have to be replaced with countries for which the null hypothesis (no relationship between revolutionary threat and working hours) is true for the result to turn insignificant. This correlation cannot be driven by any individual country or (even major) measurement error.

In Model 3, we replicate Model 2, but use our alternative measure of worker- and soldier-council movements. The result is very similar. The correlation between revolutionary threat perceptions and working hours turns out very

Table 2 Revolutionary threat in 1919 and legislated normal working hours (DV)

	(1)	**(2)**	**(3)**
Comintern invitation	−10.8***	−11.4***	
	(−5.03)	(−4.16)	
Council movement			−9.36***
			(−3.47)
Controls	No	Yes	Yes
Countries	87	87	87
R^2	0.229	0.246	0.175
Mean, hours	66.0	66.0	66.0
Min-max, hours	45–72	45–72	45–72

*$p < 0.05$, **$p < 0.01$, ***$p < 0.001$. *t*-statistics in parentheses. Restricted to countries for which we have data on main controls. Results in Model 1 are robust to including the whole sample. Control variables (log GDP p.c., log population) are omitted from table.

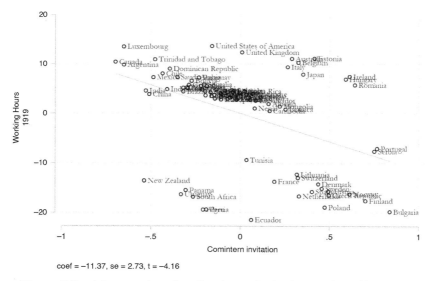

coef = −11.37, se = 2.73, t = −4.16

Figure 2 Partial regression plot: Comintern invitations and working hours
Note: The plot is based on Model 2, Table 2, and displays the controlled cross-country relationship after partialling out joint variation with Ln GDP p.c. and Ln population.

robust also to choices of temporal lags, time period under consideration, control variables, correcting standard errors for small sample bias or using jackknifed errors, and estimation technique.

To illustrate the persistence of the relationship, Figure 3 describes the development of average working hours, across time, in countries that received

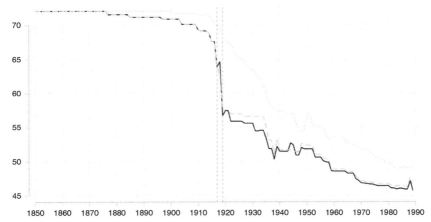

— Average working hours in countries under communistic revolutionary threat
- - Average working hours in countries under communistic revolutionary threat that existed prior to 1918
  Average working hours in countries not under communist threat

Figure 3 Average working hours in manufacturing

Comintern invitations (solid line) and those that did not (dashed line). The figure adds another (long-dashed) line for Comintern-countries, but excluding those that became independent after 1919. We observe an early divergence appearing between Comintern-invited and other countries, but their trends are still similar pre-1917; the average difference in work hours is only three hours in 1916. This difference increases to six hours in 1917, the year of the Bolshevik Revolution, and jumps further to twelve hours in 1919, when Comintern formed. This difference is still twelve hours in 1923, after which it gradually declines. A moderate difference of about three to five hours persists, however, to 1989. In Section 7, we discuss how this persistent, long-term relationship is partly mediated through Comintern participation conducing the formation of new communist parties. Where new such parties formed, lower working hours for industrial workers persisted even after the original threat of contagion of the Russian revolution dwindled.

One concern is that our estimates are driven by us setting countries with nonregulated working hours to seventy-two hours. We therefore carried out alternative regressions with instances of reform as dependent variable, coding the dummy 1 if a country introduces a working time law in 1919 that reduces the number of hours. We also construct another dummy where *any* law giving a reduction in hours in 1919 gives a 1-score. (We checked the actual date of each legislative change in 1919 and *all* changes passed parliament, or were decreed, after Comintern invitations were issued.) We then run cross-section OLS models, with our Comintern invitation measure as covariate. The results,

Table 3 Revolutionary threat and introduction of working hour law reducing work hours in 1919

	(1)	(2)	(3)	(4)
Comintern invitation	0.41***	0.41***		
	(7.82)	(4.35)		
Council movement			0.35***	0.31*
			(3.70)	(2.62)
Constant	0.017	0.037	0.359	−0.432
	(0.76)	(0.06)	(1.74)	(−0.79)
Controls	No	Yes	No	Yes
Countries	146	87	146	87
R^2	0.298	0.269	0.233	0.207
Mean dep. var.	0.089	0.149	0.089	0.149

$*p < 0.05$, $**p < 0.01$, $***p < 0.001$. t-statistics in parentheses. Linear probability (OLS) model. "Controls" are log GDP p.c. and log population.

which are similar for probit models, follow our expectations; a country facing higher revolutionary threat in 1919 is about 40 percent more likely to introduce a working time law that reduces hours, and the results (Table 3) are stable to excluding (Model 1) or including (Model 2) controls for income and population. Results are similar if we restrict our focus to countries that adopted their very first working time law in 1919. Models 3 and 4 use the presence of a worker or soldier movement in 1918–19 to proxy for revolutionary threat, and report a similar relationship.

We now turn to panel tests and once again employ our continuous measure of work hours and Comintern invitation proxy of revolutionary threat. Regarding sample composition, we always exclude Russia, since we study the threat of revolution, and not the effect of having a Communist regime. Second, we run robustness tests excluding the newly formed (post-WWI) East-European and Baltic states; these countries enter our sample before they become independent countries, without national legislation regulating working hours.[57] We also tested various starting years for our analysis, from 1789 to 1914. Since our main results remain robust to this choice (Appendix A9), we use the first year with data in most analysis to avoid selection bias and use as much information as possible to obtain good "pre-trend" estimates. As more information is included, it becomes easier to estimate whether the revolutionary threat in

---

[57] Results are robust to recoding the Baltics and Poland to have the proscribed hours of the Russian factory act of 1897, and Czechoslovakia the Austrian factory act of 1885.

1919 did, indeed, correspond with a clear and persistent break from historical trends. We use a global sample for our benchmark – the Communist revolutionary threat had global reach – but tests restricted to European countries yield similar results.

Table 4 presents results from our benchmark OLS panel regressions. Model 1 includes log GDP p.c. and log population as controls, but not the country and year dummies. This model sets the sample end year to 1925, about two years after we surmise that the revolutionary threat stemming from the Bolshevik Revolution subsided in Norway. The estimated relationship is somewhat higher than what the descriptive over-time trends in Figure 3 suggested. Specifically, the Comintern invitation dummy – which can first be scored 1 in 1919 but is then scored 1 until the time-series end in 1925 for the relevant countries – is –14.4 (hours/week), and highly significant. How sensitive is this finding? Our results would turn insignificant at the 5 percent level if 72.1 percent of observations (6,015/8,348) were replaced with "null-hypothesis observations." Any bias must be very sizeable to invalidate the result.

Yet, Figure 3 showed differences between the countries that were invited and not invited to Comintern also before 1919. Presumably, organizations from countries considered ripe for revolution were more likely to receive an invitation from Trotsky, and these countries may also have been inherently more likely to observe stricter working hour regulations. Moreover, 1919 might simply have been a fluke year, with across-the-board reductions in working hours for reasons unrelated to revolutionary threats. In Model 2, we thus add country and year dummies to mitigate such confounding. The Comintern coefficient is attenuated to 10.8 hours, which is more in line with the descriptive evidence, but remains highly significant ($t = -4.4$). The coefficient and related t-values are close to identical when entering country-specific time-trends on working hours in Model 3. In Model 4, we also add a lagged dependent variable as regressor and first-difference the dependent variable, thereby estimating a restricted Error Correction Model. The estimated *long-term coefficient* indicates a substantial reduction of -15.8 hours/week ($t = -4.3$).

In Model 5, we expand the time series to 1939, and in Model 6 to 1988, thus also capturing the longer-term relationship between Comintern invitations and working hours. This reduces the point estimate (and *t*-value) somewhat, indicating some catch-up for the "nontreated" cases towards the end of the time series. Yet, the Comintern coefficient remains at -7.5 hours/week ($t = -3.7$) even in Model 6. Finally, in Models 7 and 8, we set the time-series start year to 1900, and reestimate Models 3 and 6 (end years are 1925 and 1988, respectively). While this reduces the estimated coefficient (in Model 7) compared to Model 3 somewhat, it increases the coefficient and the precision of the estimate

Table 4 Invitation to the Comintern 1919 and legislated normal working hours

Dep var. measurement:	(1) Levels	(2) Levels	(3) Levels	(4) Changes	(5) Levels	(6) Levels	(7) Levels	(8) Levels
Comintern invitation	-14.41^{***}	-10.81^{***}	-10.71^{***}	-2.37^{*}	-8.38^{***}	-7.45^{***}	-8.41^{***}	-10.87^{***}
	(-7.01)	(-4.43)	(-4.56)	(-2.86)	(-3.67)	(-3.69)	(-3.75)	(-3.97)
Controls	Yes	Yes	Yes	Yes	Yes	Yes	Yes	Yes
Fixed effects	No	Yes	Yes	Yes	Yes	Yes	Yes	Yes
Country trends	No	No	Yes	Yes	Yes	Yes	Yes	Yes
LDV	No	No	No	Yes	No	No	No	No
Observations	8,348	8,348	8,348	8,267	9,592	15,996	2,100	9,749
Countries	105	105	105	105	105	169	92	156
Start year	1,789	1,789	1,789	1,789	1,789	1,789	1,900	1,900
End year	1,925	1,925	1,925	1,925	1,939	1,988	1,925	1,988
R^2	0.301	0.504	0.680	0.901	0.763	0.864	0.830	0.825
Mean hours	71.2	71.2	71.2	0.09	69.8	62.7	69.1	56.8
(min–max)	(45–72)	(45–72)	(45–72)	(27–3)	(40–72)	(38–72)	(45–72)	(38–72)

$*p < 0.05$, $**p < 0.01$, $***p < 0.001$. t-statistics in parentheses. OLS with errors clustered by country. Country- and year dummies, LDV (lagged dependent variable) and controls (log GDP per capita, log population) are omitted.

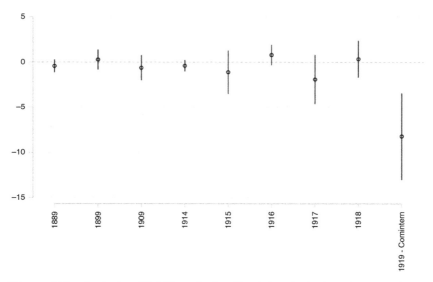

Figure 4 Placebo tests artificially assigning Comintern invitations to years prior to 1919 and reestimating Model 5, Table 4. The y-axis represents the coefficient size (i.e., the estimated relationship between Comintern invitations and work hours).

(in Model 8) when compared to Model 6. Regardless, the relationship between Comintern invitations and working hours is very robust.

We conducted several other robustness tests (Appendices A5–A9), and find similar results, for example, when using *attendance* at the first Comintern meeting. Results are also robust to various sample restrictions, such as only including European countries or countries that were independent states over the whole period.

One remaining worry – despite controls for linear country-trends and country-fixed effects – is that countries invited to Comintern were already on a particular development path, towards fewer working hours, just before they received the "treatment" in 1919. To assess this possibility, we conduct a series of placebo tests, artificially assigning Comintern invitations to the same countries, but in years prior to 1919. If these countries were already on a particular development path, these "placebo-year" Comintern dummies should remain significant predictors of lower working hours. Figure 4 draws on estimates from Model 5, Table 4, with fixed effects and country-trends, but now reestimated with Comintern participation artificially set to different years (1889, 1899, 1909, 1914–18). The results are striking; we only find a significant ($t = -3.40$) coefficient at conventional levels when measuring the treatment in 1919, and point estimates are also far smaller (with varying signs) for all other years.

Still, there could be factors that affect working time, correlate with revolutionary fear, and occur or change at the end of World War I. In Table 5, we enter controls that capture such potential confounders. These specifications extend Model 2, Table 4, with country- and year-fixed effects. (Adding country-trends does not substantially change the results.)

One important alternative explanation of social policy change is mass mobilization for war (Obinger & Petersen, 2017; Scheve & Stasavage, 2016). States with extensive mobilization in interstate war may face strong postwar demands for social policies that redistribute benefits from elites to the social groups that sacrificed lives and limbs in the war effort. This is particularly salient for us since the Bolshevik Revolution and Comintern coincided with the end of World War I. We account for the mass mobilization explanation by controlling for the percent of the population serving in the armed forces in Model 1, Table 5.[58] The Comintern coefficient only drops from 10.8 to 10.0 when including this control, and remains significant at 1 percent.

This result is supported by a more qualitative reading of our material. In Appendix A4, we provide summary tables of developments in various social policy areas, both for European countries that partook in World War I and other European countries. Several nonwarring countries that still faced revolutionary threats, such as the Netherlands and the Iberian and Scandinavian countries, expanded social policy.

In Model 2, Table 5, we control for membership in ILO, which (as Comintern) was established in 1919 and had the forty-eight-hour week as a primary goal. Rising prices could also drive labor militancy and increase the demand for reform; large food riots in Europe and Japan in 1917 originated in rising food prices. We therefore control for annual inflation (from Coppedge et al., 2021) in Model 3. Our benchmark results could also be capturing the policy effects of workers gaining political power, independent of any revolutionary threat. We thus control for reformist labor movements by including a dummy for the existence of a social democratic party in Model 4 and share of workers organized in a trade union (Rasmussen & Pontusson, 2018; interpolated) in Model 5. We control for urban industrial workers being part of the regimes' support coalition (from V-Dem) in Model 6, which should account for different types of worker influence over government. We control for whether a social democratic minister was in government in 1918–19 in Model 7, using only cross-sectional variation since the minister measure is time-invariant.

---

[58] We experimented with various ways of measuring mobilization, following Scheve and Stasavage (2016). Results are robust.

Table 5 Controlling for the most likely alternative explanations on working hours

	(1)	**(2)**	**(3)**	**(4)**	**(5)**	**(6)**	**(7)**	**(8)**
Comintern invitation	-10.00**	-9.95**	-9.74**	-9.14**	-13.2***	-10.53***	-13.36***	-9.85***
	(-3.32)	(-3.35)	(-2.97)	(-3.39)	(-3.86)	(-4.28)	(-4.29)	(-4.01)
Mobilization	-0.047							
	(-0.27)							
ILO member		-1.63						
		(-0.43)						
Inflation			-0.0018**					
			(-3.38)					
Exist. social dem. party				-0.95				
				(-1.36)				
Union density					0.11			
					(0.81)			
Regime support workers						-2.17*		
						(-2.84)		
Social democratic minister							4.74	
							(0.99)	
Electoral democracy index								-7.34*
								(-2.82)

Controls	Yes	Yes	Yes	Yes	Yes	Yes	Yes	Yes
Fixed effects	Yes	Yes	Yes	Yes	Yes	Yes	No	Yes
Observations	3,778	3,778	3,878	6,074	560	7,552	87	7,046
Countries	78	78	39	63	25	98	87	101
R^2	0.674	0.675	0.559	0.527	0.775	0.496	0.261	0.552
Mean hours	70.62	70.65	70.96	71.08	65.62	71.25	66.03	71.11
(min–max)	(45–72)	(45–72)	(45–72)	(45–72)	(45–72)	(45–72)	(45–72)	(45–72)

$*p < 0.05$, $**p < 0.01$, $***p < 0.001$. t-statistics in parentheses. OLS with standard errors clustered by country. Time series from 1817–1925 since we lack data on relevant covariates before 1817. "Controls" omitted from table are log GDP p.c. and log population. Model 7 is restricted to 1919 due to lack of minister data beyond 1919.

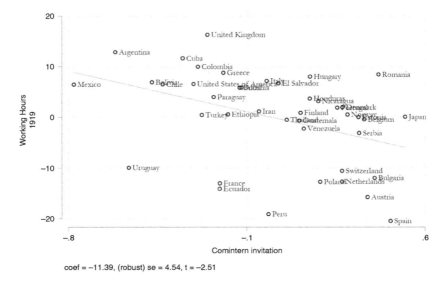

coef = −11.39, (robust) se = 4.54, t = −2.51

Figure 5 Partial regression plot: Comintern invitations and working hours
Note: The plot displays the controlled cross-country relationship after partialling out joint variation with all controls used in Table 5, except inflation and union density.

In Model 8, we include V-Dem's electoral democracy index (polyarchy). The size and significance of our Comintern measure remains robust in all tests.

In Appendix A5, we display specifications that account for other plausible alternative explanations. First, we further probe the potential role of democratic institutions, by focusing on suffrage extension (from V-Dem). In addition to total suffrage, we control for female suffrage, which may be especially relevant in our case, given possible gender differences in preferences for various public policies (e.g., Bertocchi, 2011). Second, we control for regional averages on the dependent variable to account for emulation, learning, and other mechanisms of policy diffusion from neighboring countries (Weyland, 2005). Third, since most Comintern invitations were sent to European countries, we interact a Europe dummy with a pre-/post-1919 dummy to control for the possibility that other developments in Europe drive policy shifts and generate a spurious result. Our main result is persistent, although the latter test yields insignificant results (at conventional levels) outside Europe when we include country-fixed effects. Nonetheless, the relationship is quite robust, overall: Countries with enhanced revolutionary threats after 1919 reduced the number of regulated working hours much more than other countries.

Figure 5 presents a partial-regression plot similar to in Figure 2, except that we now have included all controls in Table 5 in the model (except for union density and inflation, as their inclusion reduces the sample to 11 observations).

One remaining concern is that our regression analyses consider all nontreated countries (i.e., those that did not have unions or parties invited to Comintern) as "contrast cases"; the inclusion of less relevant cases in the control group might affect results, despite our control strategy. Thus, we construct more plausible counterfactuals to our treated cases – mixing features from several relevant, actual countries that were not invited to Comintern – by using synthetic control methods in Appendix A15. When doing so, we try to match the pre-1919 trends in work hours in our synthetic cases to those in the treated countries. We refer to Appendix A15 for these analyses and a discussion of results, and only note here that they reinforce the results from the panel models.

6.2 Instrumental Variable Regression Results

Our panel specifications control for country-fixed effects and some specifications even include country-specific trends. Yet, Comintern invitations could have been highly responsive to the perceptions of leaders in the Russian Communist Party about which countries were ripe for revolution after the dramatic and game-changing events of 1917. Lenin, Trotsky, or others might have formed judgments (based on factors not captured by our controls) about which countries were experiencing short-term developments that made them particularly likely to follow the Russian example. If so, it might be rational for Russian leaders to send Comintern invitations to unions or labor parties in exactly these countries, anticipating that this could potentially tilt the balance of scales between elites and revolutionaries. Such perceptions, formed right before or in 1919, may correlate also with the passage of social policies in 1919 or right after. To account for such endogenous selection into Comintern stemming from short-term developments, we use Zimmerwald membership (i.e., signing the proclamation of the Zimmerwald group, a breakout of radicals from the Second International in 1915, before the Bolshevik Revolution) to predict Comintern invitations. The Zimmerwald declaration, formulated by Lenin, was aimed to push worker movements towards his revolutionary line. The Zimmerwald movement's organizational arm, the International Socialist Commission (ISC), is considered a precursor to Comintern (Agnew & McDermott, 1998).

We thus use Zimmerwald membership as instrument and Comintern invitations as endogenous regressor in instrumental variable (IV) analysis. Our identifying assumption is that historical international worker radicalism – captured by Zimmerwald membership – can only influence current social policy through predicting Comintern representation, *once* we control for *current* domestic worker radicalism (we try out different such measures as controls to satisfy the exclusion restriction). We also test an alternative IV based on a similar logic, capturing which countries had actors invited to the ISC meeting in 1915.

Table 6 reports results from IV regressions (2SLS). The first-stage results show that Zimmerwald membership is a very strong predictor of Comintern invitations, passing all conventional tests for instrument strength. Further, the Comintern coefficient on working hours is larger than in our benchmark OLS specification, and various 2SLS specifications show a highly significant and robust effect. Even when we account for the possibility that (short-term) developments in revolutionary threats are causing invitations to Comintern, Comintern invitations are strongly related to subsequent changes in working hour regulations.[59]

6.3 Welfare State Coverage

So far, we have focused on working time as our outcome, but our theoretical argument and case study suggest the same relationship should be expected for various social policy outcomes preferred by the working class. First, we assess how revolutionary threat, as reflected in Comintern invitations, influenced the coverage of industrial workers in redistributive welfare programs. Given the (count) nature of these dependent variables, described in Section 5, we estimated fixed effects negative binominal count models in addition to OLS models, and results are robust. We only present the OLS results in Table 7.

The results in Table 7 follow our expectations. A higher revolutionary threat is associated with industrial workers being covered in more redistributive programs. Estimates are quite consistent when we omit (Model 1) or include (Model 2) country- and year-fixed effects, and when we add country-specific trends to the fixed effects (Model 3). Even in the latter, very restrictive model, receiving Comintern invitations in 1919 is associated with an increase in the redistributive program index (with empirical range from 0–5 programs) of about 1.5 programs. As shown in Models 4 and 5, results are robust to setting the time series start year to 1870 or 1900.

In Appendix A7, we disaggregate the dependent variable and only consider coverage of industrial workers in redistributive programs for specific risks (unemployment, sickness, etc.). Strikingly, revolutionary threat is positively associated with welfare expansion independent of which labor market or life-course risk we focus on.

---

[59] Equivalent such IV tests on other outcome variables, such as social policy coverage and generosity, show similar results.

Table 6 2SLS regressions: Invitation to the Comintern 1919 and legislated normal working hours up to 1925

	(1)	(2)	(3)	(4)	(5)
First Stage					
Zimmerwald	0.51***	0.46***	0.42***		0.22
	(13.75)	(7.21)	(5.90)		(1.93)
ISC				0.41***	0.31**
				(5.01)	(2.74)
Second Stage					
Comintern invitation	−20.80***	−17.90***	−18.10**	−14.7*	−15.90**
	(−4.74)	(−3.35)	(−2.95)	(−2.54)	(−3.14)
Mass. mob.		−0.16	−0.16	−0.14	−0.15
		(−1.13)	(−1.06)	(−0.92)	(−0.97)
ILO member		−0.15	0.35	0.24	0.28
		(−0.04)	(0.09)	(0.07)	(0.07)
Communism			1.09	0.13	0.46
			(0.37)	(0.06)	(0.21)
Reduced Form					
Zimmerwald	−10.69***	−8.32***	−7.54***		−5.27
	(−4.62)	(−3.44)	(−3.03)		(−1.74)

Table 6 (cont.)

	(1)	(2)	(3)	(4)	(5)
ISC				-6.04^{**}	-3.57
				(-2.47)	(-1.28)
Controls	Yes	Yes	Yes	Yes	Yes
Fixed effects	Yes	Yes	Yes	Yes	Yes
Observations	8,485	3,887	3,164	3,164	3,164
Countries	106	79	55	55	55
Kleibergen-Paap F	189.01	52.01	34.76	25.08	26.89
Endogenity test	4.22	2.35	2.38	1.21	2.45
	($p = 0.039$)	($p = 0.125$)	($p = 0.123$)	($p = 0.272$)	($p = 0.117$)
R^2	0.486	0.670	0.570	0.596	0.588

$^*p < 0.05$, $^{**}p < 0.01$, $^{***}p < 0.001$. t-statistics in parentheses. OLS with standard errors clustered by country. Country, year dummies, and basic controls (ln GDP p.c., ln population) omitted from table. Mass mobilization, ILO membership, and communism variables are included but not presented in first stage and reduced form.

Table 7 Invitation to the Comintern 1919 and industrial workers coverage in redistributive programs up to 1925

	(1)	(2)	(3)	(4)	(5)
Comintern invitation	2.65***	2.40***	1.74***	2.10***	1.46***
	(11.59)	(10.26)	(8.61)	(8.86)	(7.09)
Controls	Yes	Yes	Yes	Yes	Yes
Fixed effects	No	Yes	Yes	Yes	Yes
Country trends	No	No	Yes	No	No
Observations	8,350	8,350	8,350	3,898	2,103
Countries	105	105	105	96	92
Start year	1789	1789	1789	1870	1900
R^2	0.403	0.585	0.746	0.688	0.870
Mean welf. prog.	0.158	0.198	0.198	0.327	0.555
(min–max)	(0–5)	(0–5)	(0–5)	(0–5)	(0–5)

$*p < 0.05$, $**p < 0.01$, $***p < 0.001$. t-statistics in parentheses. OLS with standard errors clustered by country. Time series extend from 1817–1925. "Controls" are log GDP p.c. and log population.

7 Mechanism of Persistence: Comintern, the Formation of Communist Parties, and the Long-Term Effects of the Bolshevik Revolution

Why did the policy effect from the "Bolshevik shock" persist for so many decades, even as the shock itself dissipated? Here, we discuss one particularly plausible mechanism, pertaining to the formation of Communist parties, and present supporting evidence from cross-national tests on work-hour regulation.

Before proceeding, we point interested readers to Appendix A14, where we discuss two alternative mechanisms also relating to institutional changes (at least partly) spurred by revolutionary threat perceptions, and which shifted policymaking in a pro-worker direction. More specifically, we consider mechanisms of persistence related to suffrage extension and the adoption of PR. The tests on these alternative mechanisms of persistence are only indicative, and we warn against drawing strong conclusions from them; suffrage and electoral rules may be caused by various other factors that are hard to account for, and these features have thus changed also after the early 1920s in different countries. Yet, in Appendix A14, we elaborate on the theoretical rationale behind these potential mechanisms and report suggestive evidence that revolutionary threat around 1919 might have contributed to lower working hours even seventy

Political Economy

Table 8 Did Comintern lead to the founding of communist parties?

	(1)	(2)	(3)	(4)
Attended Comintern 1919	0.32**	0.20**	0.20*	0.24**
	(2.71)	(3.02)	(2.16)	(3.21)
Controls	Yes	Yes	Yes	Yes
Fixed effects	Yes	Yes	Yes	Yes
Country trends	No	No	Yes	Yes
Observations	5,853	6,752	6,752	9,649
End year	1925	1940	1940	1988
R^2	0.542	0.758	0.807	0.883

$*p < 0.05$, $**p < 0.01$, $***p < 0.001$. t-statistics in parentheses. Standard errors clustered by country. Dichotomous DVs measuring establishment of Communist parties. Controls are log GDP p.c. and log population.

years later due to increased likelihood of adopting PR rules. There is somewhat less clear evidence for suffrage extension being a relevant mechanism.

Did Comintern really lead to the formation of communist parties in "member countries" around the world? And, did the formation of communist parties matter for the persistence of the relationship between Comintern invitations and social policies? To answer these questions, we collected data on the year and nature of communist party formations, distinguishing between the formation of independent, new parties and the breakaway of central elements from an existing social democratic party.[60]

Model 1–2, Table 8, reports OLS regressions testing whether having attended the 1919 Comintern is associated with *establishing* a communist party, using 1925 and 1940 as time-series endpoints, with country- and year-fixed effects. (We here use Comintern attendance since the hypothesized mechanism entails domestic groups becoming embroiled with and supported by the Comintern, but results are similar for Comintern invitations.) Model 3 adds country-specific trends to Model 2, whereas Model 4 extends the time series of Model 3 to 1988. Having attended the Comintern meeting in 1919 increases the predicted probability of having a communist party by about 20–30 percentage points according to the OLS results.

We also find a clear relationship between Comintern attendance and communist parties being formed, more specifically, by a split from social democratic parties (Appendix A13).

---

[60] In Appendix A12 we list name and year of founding for all coded parties (including syndicalist parties), and whether these parties arose by breaking from a labor party.

Figure 6 Average regulated working hours, across time, for different groups of countries

There is thus a link between Comintern participation and the institutionalization of radical movements into Communist parties. Did this matter for policy developments in the long term? Figure 6 describes the development of average working hours over time for Comintern-participating and other countries. We add a long-dashed line for those Comintern countries that observed organized communist parties. Interestingly, the two sub-groups of Comintern countries track each other closely up to the late 1930s. However, starting in the 1940s, countries with communist parties had, on average, about one-to-two fewer work hours than those without. This suggests that the long-term effect of Comintern is partly mediated by the formation of Communist parties – organizations that could maintain the presence of radical forces in the country.

Still, other factors, varying between the groups of countries, could drive these differences. We therefore rerun Model 2, Table 8, but now both including and excluding the communist party variable before comparing results. We test three sample specifications in Table 9 to assess shorter- versus longer-term relationships. The time series end in 1940 in Model 1, 1960 in Model 2, and 1988 in Model 3.

The predictive power of the Comintern variable always declines when including the communist party dummy. Up to 1940, the Comintern shock is still important, as indicated by the Comintern coefficient being significant at 5 percent. In the 1960 and 1988 samples, however, the Comintern variable loses statistical significance once controlling for communist party formation.

Table 9 Long-term effect of Comintern shock when controlling or not controlling for communist parties on legislated normal working hours

End Year:	(1) 1940	(2) 1960	(3) 1988
No communist party control			
Comintern invitation	-7.07^{**}	-4.84^{*}	-4.56^{*}
	(-2.83)	(-2.16)	(-2.05)
R^2	0.754	0.828	0.864
With communist party control			
Comintern invitation	-5.84^{*}	-3.56	-2.55
	(-2.28)	(-1.62)	(-1.19)
Communist party	-3.48^{*}	-4.56^{**}	-6.79^{***}
	(-2.26)	(-2.95)	(-3.97)
R^2	0.759	0.833	0.872
Controls	Yes	Yes	Yes
Fixed effects	Yes	Yes	Yes
Observations	6,693	7,941	9,649
Countries	60	60	63

$^{*}p < 0.05$, $^{**}p < 0.01$, $^{***}p < 0.001$. t-statistics in parentheses. OLS with standard errors clustered by country. Controls are log GDP p.c. and log population.

One interpretation is that the long-term effect of the revolutionary threat-shock on work hours is mainly mediated by the formation of communist parties. The communist party variable has a strong and precisely estimated coefficient on working hours in different specifications.

In sum, our tests suggest that the formation of communist parties was one mechanism through which the "Bolshevik shock" in the late 1910s contributed to shape policy, at least in the area of work-hour regulation, even several decades later.

8 Conclusion

In this Element, we have developed a theoretical argument on how revolutionary threats that are perceived as credible by elites spur these elites to counter the threat by providing concessions in the form of social policies. We focused on the Bolshevik Revolution of 1917 and subsequent formation of Comintern in 1919, and discussed how Comintern invitations to labor parties or unions enhanced the revolutionary threat level by radicalizing the relevant movement and providing it with infrastructural and monetary support. Further, Comintern invitations functioned as information signals to elites, leading the latter to update their beliefs on how credible the revolutionary threat is. Elites responded with sticks and carrots to counter the threat, leading, for example, to expansions in social policies meant to co-opt labor.

We presented an in-depth case study of Norway after the Bolshevik Revolution and various cross-national tests to assess the extent to which revolutionary fear drove social policy development. The evidence in support of our argument is clear and robust; fear of revolution contributed to reduced working time *and* enhanced the coverage and generosity of various social transfer programs, even when accounting for several alternative explanations, and the effects seem to have persisted for decades.

We believe that our argument and findings speak to different areas of research. One example is the literature on diffusion of revolutionary threats. Here revolutionary events in neighboring countries are typically used to proxy for domestic threats, and studies mostly consider links to suffrage expansion and inequality (e.g., Aidt & Jensen, 2014; Sant'Anna & Weller, 2020). Our study is similar in many regards but focuses on policymaking. We also contribute, more specifically, by investigating the role played by the Bolshevik Revolution on the adoption and extension of various labor market- and social policies drawing on comprehensive cross-country data material.

Our theoretical contribution comes from combining a theory of how elites use social policy for co-optation purposes, with an argument on how elite perceptions of revolutionary threats are formed and influenced by international linkages to domestic groups. Other contributions study related outcomes. Obinger and Schmitt (2011) focus on regime competition and not revolutionary threat per se. Others study the direct effect of revolution (e.g., Scheidel, 2018), or focus on aspects only indirectly linked to social policy such as inequality (Sant'Anna & Weller, 2020). We provide more direct and general evidence of domestic revolutionary threat fostering social policy development. We thus add to the understanding of political factors shaping the origins of welfare states, and thus, potentially, policy determinants of redistribution and inequality (e.g., Ansell & Samuels, 2014; Boix, 2003; Iversen & Soskice, 2009; Mares, 2005; Meriläinen et al., 2021; Moene & Wallerstein, 2001; Scheidel, 2018; Scheve & Stasavage, 2009, 2016)

Finally, we contribute to the debate on how revolutionary, as opposed to reformist, labor movements shaped social policy development (e.g., Korpi, 2006; Lipset, 1983; Paster, 2013). Absent revolutionary threats, social policy was more likely to be stuck on a path in which working time went unregulated. The growth of social democratic parties, as such, was often insufficient to alter this path. But the Bolshevik Revolution, with the accompanied rise of communist parties, was a major disruptive force. Under these conditions, reformist social democrats could push for concessions, using the threat of the revolutionaries as a bargaining tool with extant elites. Future analysis of the historical role played by socialist and social democratic parties, on different types of policy developments, should thus consider and elaborate further on the role that this major international event played in altering these parties' strategies and prospects in succeeding with their policy demands.

Our study also leaves open other intriguing questions for future analysis. While our argument and case study of Norway suggests that it may be rational for elites to meet revolutionary threats with some mix of policy co-optation and repressive responses, we lack a fuller understanding of which contextual factors determine what the most appropriate mix is. Why do some elites, such as the Norwegian ones, rely heavily on carrots and implement various worker-friendly policies, whereas others rely much more heavily on repression to mitigate revolutionary threats?

We have several hypotheses. For instance, it may be that the more autocratic the regime is, the more likely elites are to rely mainly on repression. Yet, our preliminary tests do not clearly support this hypothesis. This might stem from differences in the abilities and relative costs of pursuing co-optation instead of repression for different democracies. For example, in federal democracies, where national regulation and social policy programs are difficult to implement, it may be relatively more effective to pursue repression. In extension of our argument, we also expect that it is less costly for elites to repress threats absent comprehensive unions or socialist parties that can organize an effective "backlash" challenge against the repressive elites. These speculations obviously require further theorizing and empirical study, but they could contribute to explaining why the Bolshevik threat was met by repression rather than new social policies in countries such as Japan and the United States. Insofar as they created persistent differences, understanding these divergent policy responses in the early twentieth century may even help us better understand why countries such as the United States and Norway have developed such widely different welfare states.

Finally, future studies could probe whether our argument travels to other contexts where major revolutionary events in one country created (perceptions of) significant contagion risks. While the Bolshevik Revolution was unique, especially in its global reach, other revolutions in modern history have certainly had repercussions for neighboring countries and regions. One notable such event was the late-1950s Cuban revolution, which arguably heightened perceptions of revolutionary threats, especially in Latin America (see, e.g., Weyland, 2019; Wright, 2001). Insofar as our theorized mechanisms travel, we expect the Cuban revolution to have spurred both repression and social policy development in various Latin American countries (for a relevant analysis of PRI Mexico, see Schmidt, 2008). Absent further empirical studies, we can only speculate also on this matter. Still, our guess is that the mechanisms outlined in this Element have played important roles for social policy development long after Lenin, Trotsky, and the Comintern were gone from the world stage.

References

Party and Union Documents

Arbeiderdemokraternes program (1912, 1915, 1918).

Arbeidernes Faglige Landsorganisasjon [AFL] 1918, 1919, 1920, 1921, 1923. Beretning, Oslo.

Arbeidernes Faglige Landsorganisasjon [AFL], 1918. Meddelelsesblad utgitt av Arbeidernes faglige landsorganisasjon i Norge; Christiania, No. 12.

Venstre valgprogram (1912, 1915, 1918, 1921, 1924).

Det Norske Arbeiderparti [DnA], 1918, 1919, 1920. Landsmøteprotokoll, Oslo.

Det Radikale Folkepartis valgprogram (1921, 1924).

Det Socialdemokratiske Arbeiderpartis program (1921).

Høires valgprogram (1915, 1918, 1921, 1924).

Governmental Department and Parliamentary Documents

Stortingtidende (1908, 1915, 1916, 1918, 1919, 1920, 1921, 1922, 1923). Oslo.

Stortinget (1915). Dok. nr. 49. Angaande Lov om Arbeiderbeskyttelse i industrielle virksomheter. Oslo.

Stortinget (1916). Indst. S. nr. 142. Tilraading fraa konstitutionsnemdi vedkomande grunnlovsframlegg IV og 5 C i Dok nr. 51 1914 – Forandring av § 52 D i Grunnlovi – Tap for ei tid av Røystretten ved fatighjelp. Oslo.

Stortinget (1918). Indst. O. XIV. Indstilling fra justiskomite Nr. 1 Angaande utfærdigelse av an lov om oppretholdelse av den offentlige orden og sikkerhet under krig og krigsfare. Oslo.

Stortinget (1918). Indst. O. XXIV Indst. O. XXIV. (1918) Indstilling fra socialkomiteen angaaende utfærdigelse av en midlertidig lov om forkortelse av arbeidstiden i virksomheter som omfattes av arbeiderbeksyttelsesloven. Oslo.

Stortinget (1918). Ot. prp. nr. 16. Om utfærdigelse av en lov om oppretholdelse av den offentlige orden og sikkerhet under krig og krigsfare. Oslo.

Stortinget (1918). St. prp. nr. 134. Bevilgning til Arbeiderkommisjonen. Oslo.

Stortinget (1919). Indst. S. nr. 279. Indstilling fra konstitutionskomiteen i andledning Grundlovsforslag
7 C i Dok. NR. 7 c i dok. nr. 157 for 1917, Om ophævelse av Grundlovens § 52 D – suspension av stemmeretten på grund av fattighjælp. Oslo.

Stortinget (1919). Indst. S. XXXVIII. Indstilling fra den forsterkede konstitutionskomite til forandring i Grundlovens § 57, 58, 59, 63 og 65. Oslo.

Stortinget (1919). Ot. prp. nr. 21. Om utferdigelse av en lov om forandringer i og tillegg til lov om arbeiderbeskuttelse i industrielle virksomheter av 18de september 1915. Oslo.

Stortinget (1920). Ot. prp. nr. 65. Om utferdigelse av en midlertidig lov om arbeiderutvalg i industrielle bedrifter. Oslo.

Departement for Sociale Saker (1919). Innstilling angående Normalarbeidsdag fra Komiteen av 1916 til revisjon av arbeiderbeskyttelseslovgivningen. Oslo.

Academic References

Acemoglu, D., & Robinson, J. A. (2000). Why did the West extend the franchise? Democracy, inequality, and growth in historical perspective. *Quarterly Journal of Economics, 115*(4), 1167–1199.

Acemoglu, D., & Robinson, J. A. (2006). *Economic origins of dictatorship and democracy*. Cambridge University Press.

Agøy, N. I. (1994). *Militæretaten og "den indre fiende" fra 1905 til 1940: Hemmelige sikkerhetsstyrker i Norge sett i et skandinavisk perspektiv.* Agøy.

Agøy, N. I. (1997). *Militæretaten og "den indre fiende" fra 1905 til 1940: Hemmelige sikkerhetsstyrker i Norge sett i et skandinavisk perspektiv.* University of Oslo.

Agøy, N. I. (2002). Forsvarshistorie på gyngende grunn. *Tidsskrift for samfunnsforskning, 43*(4), 587–595.

Ahmed, Amel. (2013). *Democracy and the politics of electoral system choice: engineering electoral dominance*. Cambridge University Press.

Aidt, T. S., & Jensen, P. S. (2014). Workers of the world, unite! Franchise extensions and the threat of revolution in Europe, 1820–1938. *European Economic Review, 72*, 52–75.

Alestalo, M., & Kuhnle, S. (1986). The Scandinavian route: Economic, social, and political developments in Denmark, Finland, Norway, and Sweden. *International Journal of Sociology, 16*(3–4), 1–38.

Ansell, B. W., & Samuels, D. J. (2014). *Inequality and democratization: An elite-competition approach*. Cambridge University Press.

Baldwin, P. (1988). How socialist is solidaristic social-policy: Swedish postwar reform as a case in point. *International Review of Social History, 33*, 121–147.

Baldwin, P. (1990). *The politics of social solidarity: Class bases of the European welfare state, 1875–1975*. Cambridge University Press.

Bellin, E. (2012). Reconsidering the robustness of authoritarianism in the Middle East: Lessons from the Arab Spring. *Comparative Politics, 44*(2), 127–149.

Bengtsson, E., & Molinder, J. (2017). The economic effects of the 1920 eight-hour working day reform in Sweden. *Scandinavian Economic History Review, 65*(2), 149–168.

Berman, S. (2006). *The primacy of politics: Social democracy and the making of Europe's twentieth century.* Cambridge University Press.

Bertocchi, G. (2011). The enfranchisement of women and the welfare state. *European Economic Review, 55*(4), 535–553.

Bjørgum, J. (1985). LO og NAF 1899–1940. *Tidsskrift for arbeiderbevegelsens historie, 2,* 85–114.

Bjørgum, J. (2017). Det knaker i det gamle samfunds fuger og baand. *Arbeiderhistorie, 21,* 43–63.

Bjørnson, Ø. (1990). *På klassekampens grunn: (1900–1920),* vol. 2. Tiden.

Boix, C. (2003). *Democracy and redistribution.* Cambridge University Press.

Boix, C., & Stokes, S. C. (2003). Endogenous democratization. *World Politics, 55*(4), 517–549.

Broadberry, S., Federico, G., & Klein, A. (2010). Sectoral developments, 1870–1914. In S. Broadberry & A. Klein (eds.), *The Cambridge economic history of modern Europe,* vol. 2, 59–83. Cambridge University Press.

Brooks, S. M. (2004). What was the role of international financial institutions in the diffusion of social security reform in Latin America? In K. Weyland (ed.), *Learning from foreign models in Latin American policy reform,* 53–80. John Hopkins University Press.

Cameron, D. R. (1978). The expansion of the public economy: A comparative analysis. *American Political Science Review, 72,* 1243–1261.

Carey, S. C. (2006). The dynamic relationship between protest and repression. *Political Research Quarterly, 59*(1), 1–11.

Carr, E. H. (1979). *The Russian Revolution: From Lenin to Stalin* (1917–1929). Palgrave.

Celestino, M. R., & Gleditsch, K. S. (2013). Fresh carnations or all thorn, no rose? Nonviolent campaigns and transitions in autocracies. *Journal of Peace Research, 50*(3), 385–400.

Chenoweth, E., & Belgioioso, M. (2019). The physics of dissent and the effects of movement momentum. *Nature Human Behaviour, 3*(10), 1088–1095.

Chenoweth, E., & Stephan, M. J. (2011). *Why civil resistance works: The strategic logic of nonviolent conflict.* Columbia University Press.

Collier, D., & Messick, R. E. (1975). Prerequisites versus diffusion: Testing alternative explanations of social security adoption. *American Political Science Review, 69*(4), 1299–1315.

Collier, R. B. (1999). *Paths toward democracy: The working class and elites in Western Europe and South America*. Cambridge University Press.

Coppedge, M., Gerring, J., Knutsen, C. H. et al. (2021). *V-Dem Codebook v11*. www.v-dem.net/static/website/img/refs/codebookv111.pdf.

Dahlum, S., Knutsen, C. H., & Wig, T. (2019). Who revolts? Empirically revisiting the social origins of democracy. *Journal of Politics*, *81*(4), 1494–1499.

Danielsen, R. (1984). *Borgerlig oppdemmingspolitikk: 1918–1940*, vol. 2. Cappelen forlag.

Davenport, C. (2007). State repression and political order. *Annual Review of Political Science*, *10*, 1–23.

Demirel-Pegg, T., & Rasler, K. (2021). The effects of selective and indiscriminate repression on the 2013 Gezi Park nonviolent resistance campaign. *Sociological Perspectives*, *64*(1), 58–81.

Djuve, V. L., Knutsen, C. H., & Wig, T. (2020). Patterns of regime breakdown since the French Revolution. *Comparative Political Studies*, *53*(6), 923–958.

Dobbin, F., Simmons, B., & Garrett, G. (2007). The global diffusion of public policies: Social construction, coercion, competition, or learning? *Annual Review of Sociology*, *33*, 449–472.

Eibl, F. (2020). *Social dictatorships: The political economy of the welfare state in the Middle East and North Africa*. Oxford University Press.

Emmenegger, P. (2014). *The power to dismiss: Trade unions and the regulation of job security in Western Europe*. Oxford University Press.

Esping-Andersen, G. (1990). *The three worlds of welfare capitalism*. Princeton University Press.

Esping-Andersen, G., & Korpi, W. (1986). From poor relief to institutional welfare states: The development of Scandinavian social policy. *International Journal of Sociology*, *16*(3–4), 39–74.

Estevez-Abe, M., Iversen, T., & Soskice, D. (2001). Social protection and the formation of skills: A reinterpretation of the welfare state. In P. A. Hall & D. Soskice (eds.), *Varieties of capitalism: The institutional foundations of comparative advantage*, 145–183. Oxford University Press.

Fariss, C. J., Crabtree, C. D., Anders, T. et al. (2017). Latent estimation of GDP, GDP per capita, and population from historic and contemporary sources. Working paper.

Fearon, J. D. (1995). Rationalist explanations for war. *International Organization*, *49*(3), 379–414.

Fiva, J. H., & Hix, S. (2021). Electoral reform and strategic coordination. *British Journal of Political Science*, *51*(4), 1782–1791.

Flora, P., & Heidenheimer, A. J. (1982). *The development of welfare states in Europe and America*. Transaction Books.

Fure, O.-B. (1983). *Mellom reformisme og bolsjevisme: Norsk arbeiderbevegelse 1918–1920*. Fure.

Gerschewski, J. (2013). The three pillars of stability: legitimation, repression, and co-optation in autocratic regimes. *Democratization, 20*(1), 13–38.

Gjerløw, H., & Rasmussen, M. (2022). Revolution, elite fear, and electoral institutions. *Comparative Politics, 54*(4), 595–619.

Hacker, J. S., & Pierson, P. (2002). Business power and social policy: Employers and the formation of the American welfare state. *Politics & Society, 30*(2), 277–325.

Han, K. (2021). Autocratic welfare programs, economic perceptions, and support for the dictator: Evidence from African autocracies. *International Political Science Review, 42*(3), 416–429.

Hobsbawm, E. J. (1994). *Age of extremes: The short twentieth century, 1914–1991*. Viking Penguin.

Hobson, R., & Kristiansen, T. (2001). *Norsk forsvarshistorie Bind 3: Total krig, nøytralitet og politisk splittelse 1905–1940*. Eide.

Huber, E., & Stephens, J. D. (2001). *Development and crisis of the welfare state: Parties and policies in global markets*. University of Chicago Press.

Huntington, S. P. (1991). *The third wave: Democratization in the late twentieth century*. University of Oklahoma Press.

Iversen, T. (2005). *Capitalism, democracy, and welfare*. Cambridge University Press.

Iversen, T., & Soskice, D. (2006). Electoral institutions and the politics of coalitions: Why some democracies redistribute more than others. *American Political Science Review, 100*(2), 165–181.

Iversen, T., & Soskice, D. (2009). Distribution and redistribution: The shadow of the nineteenth century. *World Politics, 61*(3), 438–486.

Iversen, T., & Soskice, D. (2019). *Democracy and prosperity*. Princeton University Press.

Johansen, S. B. (1967). *Norges samfundshjelp: Konformisme og avvik*. University of Oslo.

Knutsen, C. H., & Rasmussen, M. B. (2018). The autocratic welfare state: Old-age pensions, credible commitments, and regime survival. *Comparative Political Studies, 51*(5), 659–695.

Knutsen, P. (1994). *Korporatisme og klassekamp: Studier i forholdet mellom norsk arbeidsgiverforening, fagbevegelsen og statsmakten, 1915–1928*. University of Oslo.

Korpi, W. (1989). Power, politics, and state autonomy in the development of social citizenship: Social rights during sickness in 18 OECD countries since 1930. *American Sociological Review, 54*(3), 309–328.

Korpi, W. (2006). Power resources and employer-centered approaches in explanations of welfare states and varieties of capitalism: Protagonists, consenters, and antagonists. *World Politics, 58*(2), 167–206.

Kuhnle, S. (1978). The beginnings of the Nordic welfare states: Similarities and differences. *Acta Sociologica, 21*(1), 9–33.

Kuran, T. (1989). Sparks and prairie fires: A theory of unanticipated political revolution. *Public Choice, 61*, 41–74.

Leisering, L. (2020). The calls for universal social protection by international organizations: Constructing a new global consensus. *Social Inclusion, 8*(1), 90–102.

Lipset, S. M. (1983). Radicalism or reformism: The sources of working-class politics. *American Political Science Review, 77*(1), 1–18.

Luebbert, G. M. (1987). Social foundations of political order in interwar Europe. *World Politics, 39*(4), 449–478.

Manow, P. (2009). Electoral rules, class coalitions and welfare state regimes, or how to explain Esping-Andersen with Stein Rokkan. *Socio-Economic Review, 7*(1), 101–121.

Mares, I. (2000). Strategic alliances and social policy reform: Unemployment insurance in comparative perspective. *Politics & Society, 28*(2), 223–244.

Mares, I. (2001). Enterprise reorganization and social insurance reform: The development of early retirement in France and Germany. *Governance, 14*(3), 295–317.

Mares, I. (2003). The sources of business interest in social insurance: Sectoral versus national differences. *World Politics, 55*(2), 229.

Mares, I. (2005). Social protection around the world: External insecurity, state capacity, and domestic political cleavages. *Comparative Political Studies, 38* (6), 623–651.

Markoff, J., & White, A. (2009). The global wave of democratization. In C. W. Haerpfer, P. Bernhagen, R. F. Inglehart, & C. Welzel (eds.), *Democratization*, 55–73. Oxford University Press.

Martin, C. J., & Swank, D. (2004). Does the organization of capital matter? Employers and active labor market policy at the national and firm levels. *American Political Science Review, 98*(4), 593–611.

Martin, C. J., & Swank, D. (2012). *The political construction of business interests: Coordination, growth, and equality.* Cambridge University Press.

McDermott, K., & Agnew, J. (1996). *The Comintern: A history of international communism from Lenin to Stalin.* Macmillan.

Meriläinen, J., Mitrunen, M., & Virkola, T. (2021). The violent origins of Finnish equality. Working paper. https://papers.ssrn.com/sol3/papers.cfm? abstract_id=3741493.

Miller, M. K. (2015). Electoral authoritarianism and human development. *Comparative Political Studies*, *48*(12), 1526–1562.

Moene, K. O., & Wallerstein, M. (2001). Inequality, social insurance, and redistribution. *American Political Science Review*, *95*(4), 859–874.

Nepstad, S. E. (2013). Mutiny and nonviolence in the Arab Spring: Exploring military defections and loyalty in Egypt, Bahrain, and Syria. *Journal of Peace Research*, *50*(3), 337–349.

Nijhuis, D. O. (2009). Revisiting the Role of Labor: Worker Solidarity, Employer Opposition, and the Development of Old-Age Pensions in the Netherlands and the United Kingdom. *World Politics*, *61*(2), 296–329.

Nordvik, J. (1974). *Arbeidarrådsbevegelsen i Norge 1917–1919*. Nordvik.

Obinger, H., & Petersen, K. (2017). Mass warfare and the welfare state: Causal mechanisms and effects. *British Journal of Political Science*, *47*(1), 203–227.

Obinger, H., Petersen, K., & Starke, P. (2018). *Warfare and welfare: Military conflict and welfare state development in western countries*. Oxford University Press.

Obinger, H., & Schmitt, C. (2011). Guns and butter? Regime competition and the welfare state during the Cold War. *World Politics*, *63*(2), 246–270.

Obinger, H., & Schmitt, C. (2020). Total war and the emergence of unemployment insurance in western countries. *Journal of European Public Policy*, *27*(12), 1879–1901.

Olstad, F. (1998). Til siste kamp der gjøres klar. Planer om revolusjon i Norge i 1921. *Arbeiderhistorie*, 35–53.

Paster, T. (2013). Business and welfare state development: Why did employers accept social reforms? *World Politics*, *65*(3), 416–451.

Petersen, E. (1950). *Norsk Arbeidsgiver Forening 1900–1950*. Grøndhal & Søns boktrykkeri.

Pettersen, M. W. (2010). *Generalstaben og de revolusjonære: Revolusjonsfrykt i Generalstaben under radikaliseringen av den norske arbeiderbevegelsen i perioden 1917–1921*. Universitetet i Oslo.

Pettersen, P. A. (1987). *Pensjoner, penger, politikk*. Oslo: Universitetsforlaget.

Pons, S. (2014). *The Global Revolution: A History of International Communism 1917–1991*. Oxford University Press.

Ponticelli, J., & Voth, H.-J. (2020). Austerity and anarchy: Budget cuts and social unrest in Europe, 1919–2008. *Journal of Comparative Economics*, *48*(1), 1–19.

Przeworski, A. (2009). Conquered or granted? A history of suffrage extensions. *British Journal of Political Science*, *39*(2), 291–321.

Rasmussen, M. B. (2021). The great standardization: Working hours around the world. Working paper. University of South-Eastern Norway. www.researchgate

.net/publication/356063579_The_Great_Standardization_Working_Hours_around_the_World.

Rasmussen, M. B., & Pontusson, J. (2018). Working-class strength by institutional design? Unionization, partisan politics, and unemployment insurance systems, 1870 to 2010. *Comparative Political Studies, 51*(6), 793–828.

Rimlinger, G. V. (1971). *Welfare policy and industrialization in Europe, America, and Russia*. John Wiley & Sons.

Rueschemeyer, D., Stephens, E. H., & Stephens, J. D. (1992). *Capitalist development and democracy*. University of Chicago Press.

Sant'Anna, A. A., & Weller, L. (2020). The threat of communism during the Cold War: A constraint to income inequality? *Comparative Politics, 52*(3), 359–393.

Scheidel, W. (2018). *The great leveler*. Princeton University Press.

Scheve, K., & Stasavage, D. (2009). Institutions, partisanship, and inequality in the long run. *World Politics, 61*(2), 215–253.

Scheve, K., & Stasavage, D. (2012). Democracy, war, and wealth: Lessons from two centuries of inheritance taxation. *American Political Science Review, 106* (1), 81–102.

Scheve, K., & Stasavage, D. (2016). *Taxing the rich: A history of fiscal fairness in the United States and Europe*. Princeton University Press.

Schmidt, A. (2008). The political and economic reverberations of the Cuban Revolution in Mexico. *History Compass, 6*(4), 1140–1163.

Schmitt, C., Lierse, H., & Obinger, H. (2020). Funding social protection: Mapping and explaining welfare state financing in a global perspective. *Global Social Policy, 20*(2), 143–164.

Schmitt, C., Lierse, H., Obinger, H., & Seelkopf, L. (2015). The global emergence of social protection: Explaining social security legislation 1820–2013. *Politics & Society, 43*(4), 503–524.

Skorge, Ø. S., & Rasmussen, M. B. (2021). Volte-face on the welfare state: Social partners, knowledge economies, and the expansion of work–family policies. *Politics & Society*. OnlineFirst.

Sørensen, Ø., & Brandal, N. (2018). Det norske demokratiet og dets fiender, 1918–2018. Dreyers.

Soskice, D. W., & Hall, P. A. (2001). *Varieties of capitalism: The institutional foundations of comparative advantage*. Oxford University Press.

Strang, D., & Chang, P. M. Y. (1993). The International Labor Organization and the welfare state: Institutional effects on national welfare spending, 1960–80. *International Organization, 47*(2), 235–262.

Sullivan, C. M. (2016). Undermining resistance: Mobilization, repression, and the enforcement of political order. *Journal of Conflict Resolution, 60*(7), 1163–1190.

Sullivan, C. M., & Davenport, C. (2017). The rebel alliance strikes back: Understanding the politics of backlash mobilization. *Mobilization*, *22*(1), 39–56.

Sundvall, E. W. (2017). Arbeiderpartiet og klassekrigen: Striden om Moskvatesene i 1920 i en internasjonal kontekst. *Arbeiderhistorie*, *21*(1),65–83.

Swank, D., & Martin, C. J. (2001). Employers and the welfare state: The political economic organization of firms and social policy in contemporary capitalist democracies. *Comparative Political Studies*, *34*(8), 889–923.

Swenson, P. (1991a). Bringing capital back in, or social-democracy reconsidered: Employer power, cross-class alliances, and centralization of industrial relations in Denmark and Sweden. *World Politics*, *43*(4), 513–544.

Swenson, P. (1991b). Labor and the limits of the welfare-state: The politics of intraclass conflict and cross-class alliances in Sweden and West Germany. *Comparative Politics*, *23*(4), 379–399.

Swenson, P. (1997). Arranged alliance: Business interests in the New Deal. *Politics & Society*, *25*(1), 66–116.

Swenson, P. (2002). *Capitalists against markets: The making of labor markets and welfare states in the United States and Sweden*. Oxford University Press.

Swenson, P. (2004). Varieties of capitalist interests: Power, institutions, and the regulatory welfare state in the United States and Sweden. *Studies in American Political Development*, *18*(1), 1–29.

Tranmæl, M. (1913). *Hvad fagoppositionen vil*. Trondhjem.

Therborn, G. (1984). Classes and States Welfare State Developments, 1881–1981. *Studies in Political Economy*, *14*(1), 7–41.

Trotsky, L. (2022, 22 October). Letter of Invitation to the Congress 24 January 1919. www.marxists.org/history/international/comintern/1st-congress/invitation.htm?fbclid=IwAR2oLTBT4q89HDUSmawig dOsnhQSTl1qAKS_gRnhly5r42z5yKy2oQ9GgYs.

Vis, B. (2019). Heuristics and political elites' judgment and decision-making. *Political Studies Review*, *17*(1), 41–52.

Weyland, K. (2005). Theories of policy diffusion lessons from Latin American pension reform. *World Politics*, *57*(2), 262–295.

Weyland, K. (2010). The diffusion of regime contention in European democratization, 1830–1940. *Comparative Political Studies*, *43*(8–9), 1148–1176.

Weyland, K. (2014). *Making waves: Democratic contention in Europe and Latin America since the revolutions of 1848*. Cambridge University Press.

Weyland, K. (2019). *Revolution and reaction*. Cambridge University Press.

Wintrobe, R. (1998). *The political economy of dictatorship*. Cambridge University Press.

Wright, T. C. (2001). *Latin America in the era of the Cuban Revolution*. Greenwood.

Xu, R, Frank, K. A., Maroulis, S. J., & Rosenberg, J. M. (2019). Konfound: Command to quantify robustness of causal inferences. *Stata Journal, 19*(3), 523–550.

Young, L. E. (2019). The psychology of state repression: Fear and dissent decisions in Zimbabwe. *American Political Science Review, 113*(1), 140–155.

Cambridge Elements ☰

Political Economy

David Stasavage
New York University

David Stasavage is Julius Silver Professor in the Wilf Family Department of Politics at New York University. He previously held positions at the London School of Economics and at Oxford University. His work has spanned a number of different fields and currently focuses on two areas: development of state institutions over the long run and the politics of inequality. He is a member of the American Academy of Arts and Sciences.

About the Series

The Element Series Political Economy provides authoritative contributions on important topics in the rapidly growing field of political economy. Elements are designed so as to provide broad and in-depth coverage combined with original insights from scholars in political science, economics, and economic history. Contributions are welcome on any topic within this field.

Cambridge Elements ≡

Political Economy

Milton Keynes UK
Ingram Content Group UK Ltd.
UKHW051813181223
R3472600001B/R34726PG434567UKX00002B/1